United States History

Workbook

POWER BASICS PLUS

Project Staff

Writer .... Hilarie Staton

Editorial .... Susan Blair
Maggie Jones
Elizabeth Lynch
Richard Lynch
Holly Moirs
Kate O'Halloran
Mary Rich
Erica Varney

Art and Design .... Roman Laszok
Sheila Russell
Mark Sayer
Ian Weidner

1 2 3 4 5 6 7 8 9 10

ISBN 0-8251-5665-3

J. Weston Walch, Publisher
P. O. Box 658 • Portland, Maine 04104-0658
walch.com

Printed in the United States of America

Table of Contents

Table of Contents, *continued*

Table of Contents, *continued*

To the Student

Welcome! This *Power Basics® United States History Workbook* is designed to be used with your *Power Basics® United States History* student text. Each activity will help reinforce, extend, or enrich the material in your textbook.

Reinforcement activities provide practice in what you have learned in the student text. These activities may be very similar to those in the textbook, or they may take a different approach to the content.

Extension activities include a number of different approaches to the material and may "extend" the information a bit further. They may include critical-thinking questions, research questions, or real-life applications. In some cases, information that is covered briefly in the text is developed further in the extension activities.

Since everyone learns in a different way, activities that invite the multiple intelligences are also included in this workbook. These activities help you connect to the material through approaches such as physical movement, partner and group dialogue and games, and visual respresentations.

Power Basics® is designed to give you the foundation you need to do well in school and beyond. This workbook builds on the material you have learned in the student text and gives you a solid skills base to help you meet your academic and other goals.

NAME:

UNIT 1 • ACTIVITY 1
Native American Life

Many American Indians lived in North America. They were here long before the European explorers came. American Indian nations used their environment to meet their needs and wants.

Choose a North American Indian culture. The people might have lived in the Northern Woodlands, Southeast, Southwest, Northwest, or on the Great Plains.

Find information about how the people of this culture lived. Use the organizer and questions below. They will help you take notes and organize your information.

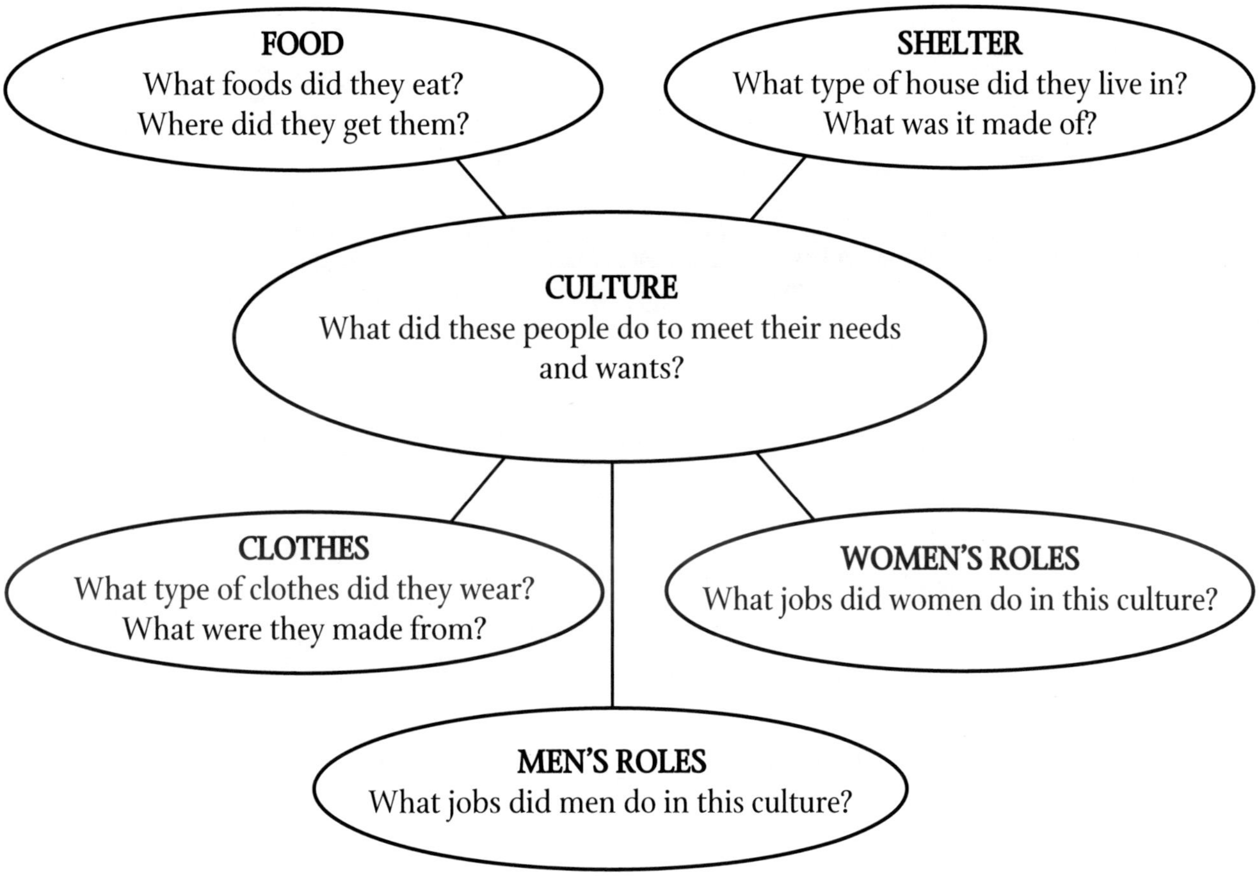

FOOD
What foods did they eat?
Where did they get them?

SHELTER
What type of house did they live in?
What was it made of?

CULTURE
What did these people do to meet their needs and wants?

CLOTHES
What type of clothes did they wear?
What were they made from?

WOMEN'S ROLES
What jobs did women do in this culture?

MEN'S ROLES
What jobs did men do in this culture?

Choose a way to present your findings to others. Show how these people met their needs and wants.

- Draw a picture.
- Write a description.
- Act out a scene.

NAME:

UNIT 1 • ACTIVITY 2
Important Colonial Terms

Use a word listed in the box to correctly complete each sentence.

Native Americans	England	Puritans
colonists	explorers	religious freedom
conflicts	India	taxes
culture	New World	voyage

1. The ______________________ were looking for a short route to India.

2. They found ______________________ living in North America.

3. Europeans called America the ______________________.

4. People from ______________________ settled the east coast of North America.

5. The ______________________ made their homes in the new land but were still ruled by their native countries.

6. To get to America, colonists had to make a long, difficult ______________________.

7. Some people came to America looking for ______________________.

8. One English religious group, the ______________________, settled in Massachusetts.

9. Some people came to America to escape high ______________________.

10. There were many ______________________ between Native Americans and Europeans.

11. Many different groups of Native Americans lived in America, and each had its own ______________________ and language.

12. European explorers came upon America while looking for a shorter route to ______________________.

UNIT 1 • ACTIVITY 3
Colonial Life

Many colonists came to America. Most were farmers. Some were craftspeople, such as blacksmiths or printers. Some were traders or merchants. People brought many customs with them. They also had to adapt to a new place. In America, they had a different life than the one they had lived in Europe.

Work with a few students. As a group, choose two of the families listed below. Find out about the life of these families. Fill in the chart with what you find. Then work with your group to create a skit. In the skit, one family should meet the other family. The families should talk about how their lives are different and the same.

Choose two families listed in the box.

Puritan family	Dutch merchant's family in New York City	plantation family
Pennsylvania Quaker family	Spanish family in St. Augustine, Florida	small farmer's family in eastern Virginia
craftsperson's family in Boston	slave family	New England fishing family
French family in Quebec		

	Homes	Customs and Language	Religious Activities	Jobs	Daily Activities
Family 1:					
Family 2:					

NAME:

UNIT 1 • ACTIVITY 4
Colonial Workers

Read about colonial workers. Then answer the questions. Use complete sentences.

Life in the colonies was filled with things to do. Workers were scarce in the colonies. *Scarce* means "hard to find." Most colonists who needed help could not find workers to hire. Most people who came to the colonies began their own farms. They did not want to work for anyone else.

Some colonists had indentured servants. Indentured servants were people who wanted to come to the colonies but could not pay for the trip. They agreed to work seven years without pay. In exchange, the person who hired them paid their way to America. Indentured servants also received a place to live, food to eat, and clothes to wear. They had to work very hard and did not have much time or money of their own.

Many colonists owned slaves. Most slaves were captured in Africa. They were brought to the colonies in chains. They were sold to colonists and treated as property. They worked for their owners, who fed them and gave them clothes. Some owners treated their slaves well, but some were very cruel. No slave became free unless he or she was given their freedom by their owner, bought their freedom, or ran away.

1. What does *scarce* mean?

   ____

2. What was scarce in the colonies?

   ____

3. What was an indentured servant?

   ____

4. What happened to an indentured servant after seven years?

   ____

5. How did slaves get to the colonies?

   ____

6. How were slaves treated by their owners?

   ____

7. What were some differences between indentured servants and slaves?

   ____

8. Why do you think indentured servants and slaves sometimes ran away?

   ____

NAME:

UNIT 1 • ACTIVITY 5
Colonial Trade

The chart below shows some of the major exports of the Thirteen Colonies. An export can be raw materials or finished goods. Exports are sent to another country for sale or trade.

Use the information in the chart to answer the questions.

	Farm goods	Forest goods	Sea goods	Finished goods
New England colonies	wool, dried meat	lumber, trees for masts	fish, whale products	rum, ships
Middle colonies	flax, cattle and meat, corn, wheat	fur		barrels, rum, flour
Southern colonies	tobacco, indigo, rice	tar, pitch, lumber		

1. Which colonies used the ocean to get some of its exports?

2. Which colonies exported the widest variety of food products?

3. Which colonies did not export any finished goods?

4. Compare the exports of the New England colonies with those of the Middle colonies.

5. Compare the exports of the Southern colonies with those of the other colonies.

6. What factors do you think explain the differences among the exports of the different colonies?

NAME:

UNIT 1 • ACTIVITY 6
The Road to War

The events listed in the box happened before the American Revolution. Some events made the British government angry with the colonists. Some events made the colonists angry with the British government. Research each event. Write each event in the sentence that tells about it.

Boston Massacre	French and Indian War	Stamp Act
Boston Tea Party	Intolerable Acts	Townsend Acts
First Continental Congress	Proclamation of 1763	

1. After the British won the ______________________________, they took control of Canada.

2. The ______________________________ said that colonists could not move west of the Appalachian Mountains. The British did not want to protect the settlers from the American Indians living there.

3. The ______________________________ made colonists angry. They did not want taxation without representation. They called a meeting of people from all the colonies.

4. The British were upset that the colonists were trading with other countries. The British passed the ______________________________ to control colonial trade.

5. Many colonists were angry with the British. Some threw stones at British soldiers. The British soldiers fired into the crowd. This was the ______________________________.

6. The British said only one British company could sell tea in the colonies. The colonists held the ______________________________ to show their anger at that rule.

7. The ______________________________ were meant to punish the colonists in Massachusetts.

8. The colonists were very angry about how the British government was treating them. Their representatives met at the ______________________________. They discussed what should be done.

NAME:

UNIT 1 • ACTIVITY 7
The Loyalists and the Patriots

During the American Revolution, people took sides. Loyalists wanted the colonies to stay under the British government. Patriots wanted an independent government for the colonies.

Read each statement below. Some are what a Loyalist might say. Some are what a Patriot might say. After each statement, write *Loyalist* or *Patriot* to show who might say it.

1. England is our mother country. We should follow England's laws. ________________

2. We want to decide our own taxes and how to spend them. We do not want taxation without representation. ________________

3. The English government would not force people in London to do this. Why should we let soldiers live with us? ________________

4. We need the British navy to protect our trading ships. ________________

5. If this country gets independence, the new government will take away all the land I own. ________________

6. The British government is not treating us as equals. They do not deserve to profit from our trade. ________________

7. Our colonies have governed themselves for many years. Why should England take control now? ________________

8. No colonists are in Parliament. No one represents us in that legislature. ________________

9. My job is with the British government. I do not want to lose it. ________________

10. Colonial governments did not give us full rights because of our religion. Maybe a new government would give us full rights. ________________

NAME:

UNIT 1 • ACTIVITY 8
Problems Puzzle

There were many problems during the time the United States was governed by the Articles of Confederation. Use the words listed in the box to complete the sentences about these problems.

borders	inflation	Rebellion
confederation	legislature	Revolution
debts	money	states
governor	navy	tax

1. A(n) ____________ is a group that joins together for a purpose but stay independent.
2. Before the Articles of Confederation were accepted, a(n) ____________ ran each colony.
3. Under the Articles of Confederation, each state ____________ elected people to Congress.
4. Some states fought over where their ____________ were located.
5. During the American ____________, Congress wrote the Articles of Confederation.
6. America had 13 ____________ under the Articles of Confederation.
7. Shays' ____________ was about judges sending people to jail when they could not pay their debts.
8. America had high ____________, so prices rose quickly and people could not pay their debts.
9. ____________ was not worth as much as it had been before the war.
10. The government owed many ____________, but the states would not give it enough money to pay them.
11. The new country had no army or ____________ for protection.
12. Only a state could make people pay ____________.

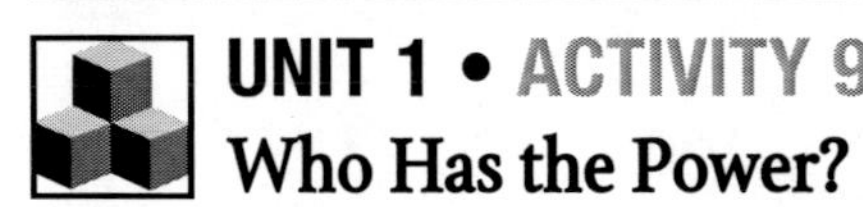

UNIT 1 • ACTIVITY 9
Who Has the Power?

The Articles of Confederation divided power between the national government and the state governments. Power was divided differently from the way it is today.

Listed in the box are some government powers. Write each one in the chart. Write it under the National government if it was a power of the national government or Congress. Write it under State government if it was a power of the state governments. Then answer the question at the bottom using the information in the chart.

conduct foreign policy	control commerce and trade	collect taxes
declare war	write treaties with other countries	enforce laws
issue currency	settle disagreements between states	

National government	State governments

Did the Articles of Confederation create a weak national government? Support your answer with examples from the chart.

____

____

____

____

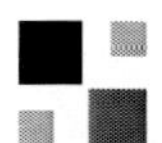

NAME:

UNIT 1 • ACTIVITY 10
Philadelphia: A Busy City

Philadelphia was an important city when the Constitutional Convention met there. It was filled with craftspeople, tradespeople, farmers, and businesspeople. Choose one type of business found in 1787 Philadelphia. Investigate the jobs, goods, and activities related to that business. Answer these questions about the business.

Business: ______________________________

1. What jobs did people do in this business? ______________________________

____

2. What services did the business provide for people? ______________________________

____

3. What goods were made or sold by the business? ______________________________

____

After you know about your business, write a short speech. As you give your speech to the class, imagine you are speaking to the representatives at the Constitutional Convention. Tell them why they should do business with you while they are in your city.

____

____

____

Use what you have heard from classmates to describe three other Philadelphia businesses that you think the Convention Representatives should use.

____

____

____

NAME:

UNIT 1 • ACTIVITY 11
The Constitution's Powers

The United States has a Constitution. It tells how the government is organized. Both the state governments and the federal government have some powers. The chart below lists the types of powers. Define each type of power, then write two examples of that type of power.

Type of powers	Definition	Two examples
Expressed powers		1. 2.
Implied powers		1. 2.
Reserved powers		1. 2.
Concurrent powers		1. 2.

NAME:

UNIT 1 • ACTIVITY 12
Plantation Life

Many people lived on a plantation. The plantation owner and his family lived in a large house. Many were rich and had furniture imported from Europe. Large plantations had an overseer. His job was to oversee, or watch over, slaves who worked in the fields. Plantations grew mostly cash crops. They grew tobacco, cotton, indigo, and rice to sell. Slaves worked in the fields. They also cleaned and cooked for the owner's family. Some slaves were taught skills, such as weaving and blacksmithing.

Think about all the jobs that were done on a plantation. Then read the conversations below. What are the roles of the two people talking? Write a role listed in the box to show who says which line.

plantation owner	overseer	field slave	house slave

1. "You must have that tobacco field planted by sunset. Get to work!" said the

   ____________________.

   "Yes, but it is so hot I cannot work very fast," answered the ____________________.

2. "I will be taking my family to spend the summer in Charleston," said the ____________________.

   "I will make sure the slaves gather the crops," said the ____________________.

3. "Please do not make my children work in the rain today," begged the ____________________.

   "Every worker will do their part, no matter what his or her age," replied the

   ____________________.

4. "The party will be for 50 people. I think 30 will be spending the night," stated the

   ____________________.

   "What do you want me to make for dinner and breakfast?" asked the ____________________.

5. "Working in the kitchen is hard. Someone is always watching you," sighed the

   ____________________.

   "Working in the fields is harder work, but I like the fresh air and quiet there," said the

   ____________________.

NAME:

UNIT 1 • ACTIVITY 13
Federalists and Antifederalists

The Constitution was written. Then it had to be ratified. *Ratify* means "to approve." Nine of the 13 states had to ratify the Constitution. After that the new government could start. Each state held a ratification convention. Famous Americans, farmers, tradesmen, and local politicians went to them.

Federalists supported the Constitution. They wanted a federal system with a strong central government. The Federalists all agreed. They wanted the states to ratify the Constitution.

Antifederalists did not support the Constitution for many different reasons. Many Antifederalists feared a strong national government. They believed this would take away a state's power. Some were upset that the Constitution did not have a bill of rights. Some were unhappy that it did not protect slavery. Others were unhappy that it did not end slavery. Some felt the Constitutional Convention did not have the power to create a whole new government. There were many other issues, too. Antifederalists agreed on only one thing. They did not want the Constitution to be ratified.

Find facts about the Federalists and the Antifederalists. Find out about each side's arguments. Create a two-sided poster. On one side, use pictures, words, and phrases for a Federalist's argument. Try to convince people to ratify the Constitution. On the other side, use pictures, words, and phrases for an Antifederalist's argument. Try to convince people not to ratify the Constitution.

In the space below, brainstorm your poster ideas before you begin creating it.

Federalist	Antifederalist

NAME:

UNIT 1 • ACTIVITY 14
The Amendment Process

The writers of the Constitution included a way to change it. They did not make this easy. They wanted only important changes made. Amendments are additions that change the Constitution. Twenty-seven amendments have been passed.

Here are the steps for changing the Constitution. These steps must be followed. Two different sets of steps can be used. One of these methods has never been used.

Read the steps. Then answer the questions below.

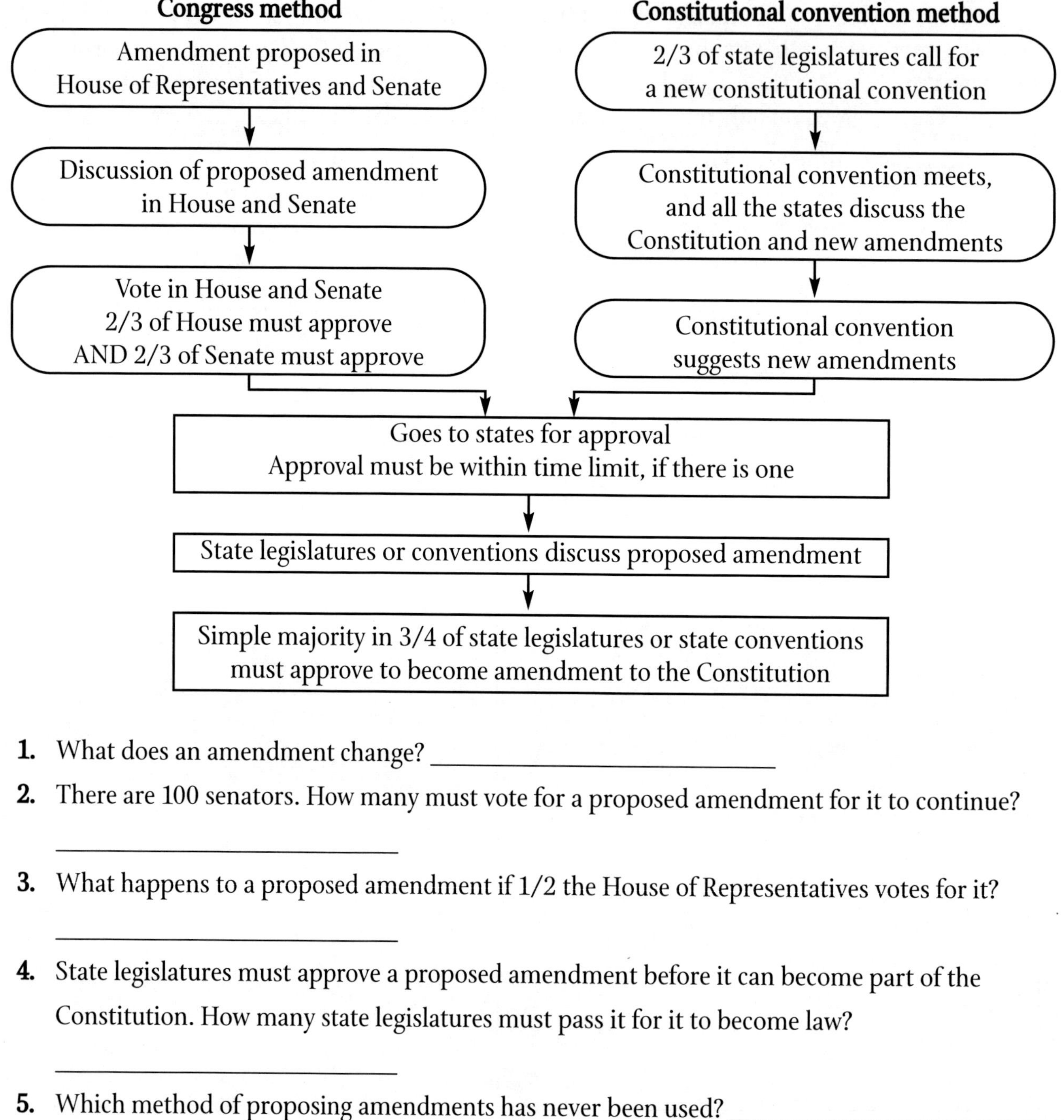

1. What does an amendment change? ______________________

2. There are 100 senators. How many must vote for a proposed amendment for it to continue?

    ____

3. What happens to a proposed amendment if 1/2 the House of Representatives votes for it?

    ____

4. State legislatures must approve a proposed amendment before it can become part of the Constitution. How many state legislatures must pass it for it to become law?

    ____

5. Which method of proposing amendments has never been used? ______________________

NAME:

UNIT 1 • ACTIVITY 15
Government Terms

There are many special terms used to talk about the government and the Constitution. The terms below are important. A list of definitions appears below the box. Cut out each definition and glue it onto an index card. On the other side of the card, write the word from the box that it defines. Check with a partner to make sure your terms and definitions are correct. Then play a matching game using both sets of cards. Place one set out with the words up. Place the other set out with the definition up. Then take turns matching terms and their definitions.

amendments	Bill of Rights	separation of powers
Constitution of the United States	executive branch	cabinet
democracy	judicial branch	
legislative branch	checks and balances	

This branch of government includes the House of Representatives and Senate.

This is the highest law in the United States. It describes the American government.

This type of government is run by the people who live under it.

These are how the Constitution makes sure one branch of the government does not become too powerful.

These are changes to the U. S. Constitution.

This branch of government is responsible for carrying out the laws. It is headed by the president.

This is the division of duties and powers between the branches of government.

This group advises the president.

This lists the rights of all people. It is made up of the first ten amendments to the Constitution.

This branch of government is responsible for interpreting the law. It includes the courts and judges.

NAME:

UNIT 1 • ACTIVITY 16
The Judicial Branch

The judicial branch is one branch of the federal government. It includes the courts and judges. There are two judicial systems in the United States. One is the federal court system. The other is the state system. The court system in each state is a little different.

Below is a chart of the federal court system. Find information about your state's court system. Use that information to create a chart like this one. Then use it to answer these questions.

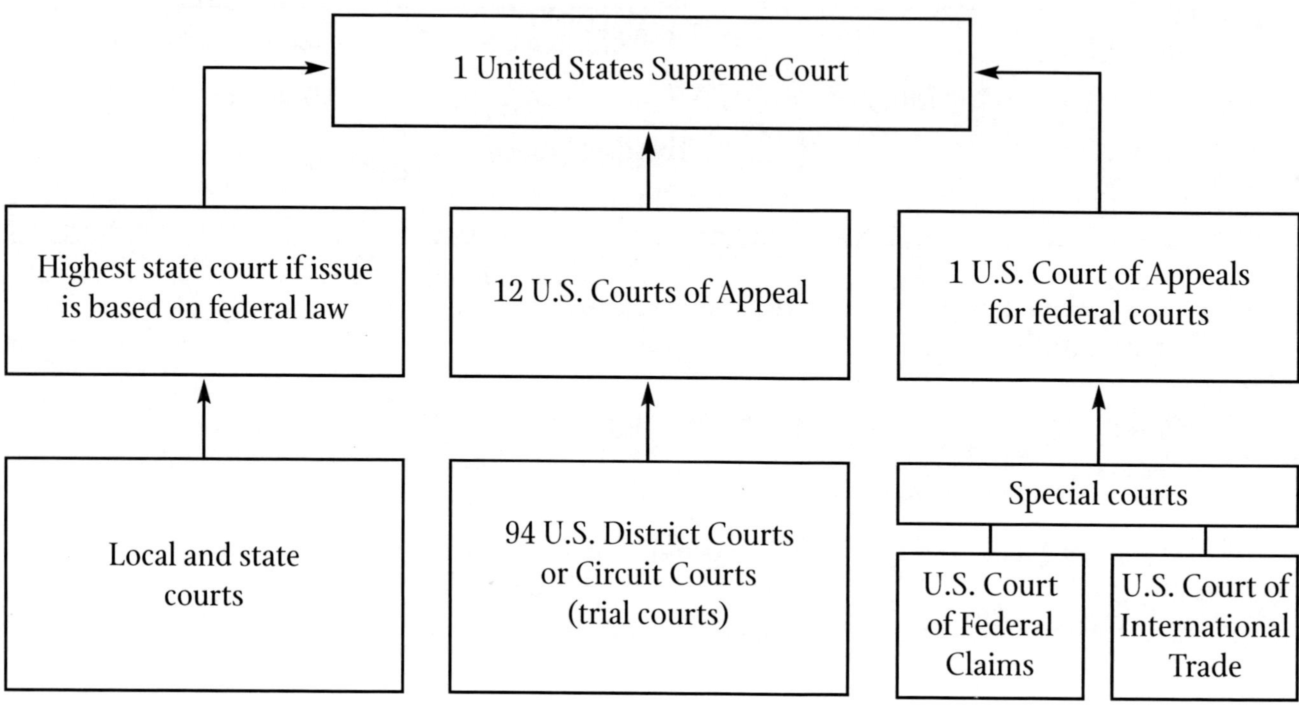

1. What is the highest court in the United States? ______________________

2. What is the highest court in your state? ______________________

3. In which state courts do cases usually start? ______________________

4. What are your state's courts of appeal called? ______________________

5. What are your local courts? ______________________

NAME:

UNIT 1 • ACTIVITY 17
The Birth of American Political Parties

At first, the United States did not have political parties. Then people began to vote for different candidates because of what they believed. This is how political parties began. When political parties became powerful, the government had to change.

Read the paragraphs. Use the words from the box to fill in the blanks.

president	Republican	team
Constitution	political party	Congress
Republicans	vice president	
Federalist	constitutional amendment	

The way a president is elected has changed. The **1.** _________________ did not allow for political parties. It said the person who is running for president with the most votes will be **2.** _________________. The one with the next highest number of votes will be **3.** _________________.

In 1796, John Adams was elected president. He was a **4.** _________________. His vice president was Thomas Jefferson. He was a **5.** _________________. This was the only time a president and vice president did not belong to the same **6.** _________________.

In 1800, Thomas Jefferson ran for president. Aaron Burr ran for vice president. They were both **7.** _________________. They both received the same number of votes. So there was a tie for president. **8.** _________________ had to break the tie. They voted many times. Finally, Thomas Jefferson received more votes. He became president. Aaron Burr became vice president.

Congress did not want a tie between people from the same party again. They passed a **9.** _________________. It changed the way a president is elected. Now a president and a vice president are elected as a **10.** _________________. The pair that has the most electoral votes wins.

NAME:

UNIT 2 • ACTIVITY 18
Frontier Life

Read these questions. Find information about living on the frontier. Answer each question in a complete sentence.

1. What is a wilderness? ____________________
2. What did settlers eat when they first arrived to settle in a place in the wilderness? ____________________
3. How did settlers build a log cabin? ____________________
4. What did settlers do to the forests to begin their farms? ____________________
5. Why did frontier settlers have to reuse items, such as clothes? ____________________
6. Where did settlers get their furniture? ____________________
7. What happened to an area to change it from a wilderness to a frontier? ____________________
8. How did frontier settlers help one another? ____________________
9. Why were most frontier settlers happy to see travelers? ____________________
10. Would you have liked to be a frontier settler? Why or why not? ____________________

NAME:

UNIT 2 • ACTIVITY 19
Lewis and Clark's Journey

President Jefferson bought the Louisiana Territory. He got a good deal, but he did not know much about the land. He sent a team to explore it. Meriwether Lewis and William Clark traveled across this wilderness. They found plants and animals that scientists had never seen. They had to cross many types of land and water. They kept journals as they traveled. They used both words and pictures to describe what they saw. They were gone for two years. They brought back plants and animals. They published their journals.

Find information about one event on Lewis and Clark's journey. Write a journal entry about it. Draw a picture of the plants, animals, or landforms that were part of that event. Read the journal entry to others in your class. Discuss the things Lewis and Clark saw and did and some of the problems they faced.

JOURNAL

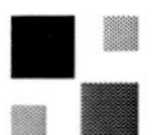

NAME:

UNIT 2 • ACTIVITY 20
Early Trade with the United States

Goods are made, produced, or grown in a country. These goods might be sent to another country, or exported. They are sold in that country. When one country brings in goods from another, the goods are imported. The United States exports, or sends, goods to Canada. The United States imports, or gets, goods from China. The graphs below show the exports from and imports to the United States. Use the graph and what you know about the United States to answer the questions.

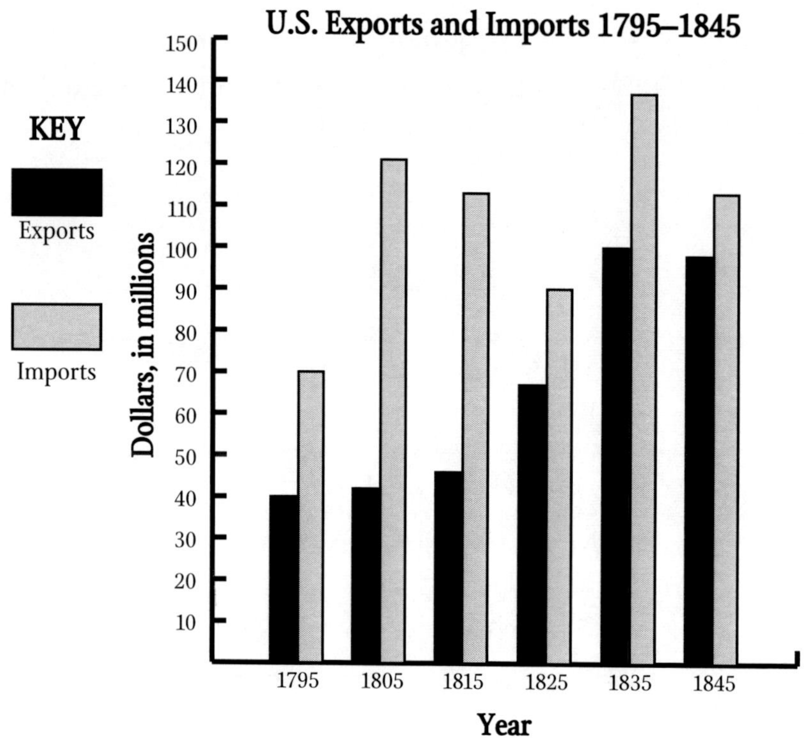

1. What was the value of exports of U. S. products in 1805? ______________________

2. Between what years was the biggest growth in U.S. exports? ______________________

3. Which year had the biggest difference between the value of imported goods and exported goods? ______________________

4. What war slowed imports and exports between 1805 and 1815? ______________________

5. What new way of moving goods helped increase exports between 1825 and 1835?

____

6. Most American exports were farm goods. What crops were the most important American exports? ____

NAME:

UNIT 2 • ACTIVITY 21
Who Said It?

Read the following statements. Decide which person or group of people listed in the box would have made each statement. Write the name of the correct person or group on the line.

Dolley Madison	British military	Canadians
President James Madison	Northwestern frontier farmers	Thomas Jefferson
French government	Native Americans	Lewis and Clark
American merchants		

1. Americans must stop sending their export goods to New Orleans!

 ____

2. We should buy this land from France, for it will double the size of our country.

 ____

3. We are exploring a wild and beautiful land. It is very different from where most Americans live.

 ____

4. We need to ship this wheat down the Mississippi River. When it reaches New Orleans, we can sell it. ____________________

5. If we had more guns, we would fight the American settlers moving into the Northwest Territory! ____________________

6. We want to trade with both the British and the French. We cannot do so if they keep taking our ships. ____________________

7. I read the report from the Navy. We cannot let this continue! I will ask Congress to declare war on Great Britain! ____________________

8. We will not join the United States in its fight against the British.

 ____

9. We must leave the White House quickly. The president said the British Army will be here soon.

 ____

10. We have burned their capital! ____________________

NAME:

UNIT 2 • ACTIVITY 22
Working Together on the Frontier

More and more settlers moved to the frontier. People lived closer to other people. They helped one another do things that were hard or boring to do alone.

In a small group, find out what happened at one of the events listed in the box. Answer the questions below with facts about the event. Use those facts to plan a presentation. Present your information to the class. You might present it as a skit, a series of pictures, a story, or a dialog in letters.

quilting bee	house raising	corn husking	harvesting grain

1. Which event did you choose? ____________________

____

2. What was the purpose of the event? ____________________

____

3. What did people do to get ready for the event? ____________________

____

4. What different things did people do at this event? ____________________

____

5. What was the result of the event? ____________________

____

In the space below, brainstorm ideas about your presentation.

NAME:

UNIT 2 • ACTIVITY 23
The Erie Canal

New transportation changed America in many ways. It changed American business. It also changed where people lived. Many people moved to be near the transportation. Some wanted to use the transportation. Most wanted jobs. Some of these jobs were in transportation. Some were in the factories and businesses that opened in the cities near the transportation.

Here is a chart that shows the growth of three cities along the Erie Canal. Use it to answer the questions below.

Population in Cities Along the Erie Canal from 1810 – 1860

	1810	1820	1830	1840	1850	1860
Albany	10,762	12,630	24,209	33,721	50,763	62,367
Rochester			9,207	20,191	36,403	48,235
Buffalo			8,668	18,213	42,261	81,129

1. Which cities did not exist in 1820? ______________________________

2. What was the population of Albany in 1820? ______________ In 1830? ______________

3. What happened to Rochester and Buffalo between 1820 and 1830? ______________

4. Why did these cities grow so fast after 1830? ______________

5. How much did Albany grow between 1810 and 1860? ______________

6. How much did Rochester grow between 1830 and 1860? ______________

7. How much did Buffalo grow between 1830 and 1860? ______________

8. What city grew the most between 1830 and 1860? ______________ Why do you think that happened? Support your opinion with facts. ______________

____

____

9. What do you think you would find in Rochester in 1860 that was not there in 1830? ______________

____

10. How did the Erie Canal affect these cities? ______________

____

NAME:

UNIT 2 • ACTIVITY 24
Andrew Jackson

Many people did not agree with President Andrew Jackson. The chart below lists issues and events from his time. Find out about each topic in your textbook, in an encyclopedia, or on the Internet. Take notes in the chart below. Describe the issue or event. Tell how it affected Americans. Then write your opinion about what happened. Support it with facts about the event and its results.

	Describe the issue and/or event.	What effect did this issue or event have on people?	What is your opinion on the issue? Support it with details.
Expanding suffrage			
Spoils system			
Trail of Tears			
Tariffs and nullification			
Jackson's war on banks			

NAME:

UNIT 2 • ACTIVITY 25
Before the Civil War

Read each sentence below. Use the words listed in the box to complete each sentence. Write your choice in the puzzle. Then complete the last sentence with the mystery word.

1 ___ ___ ___ ___ ___

2 ___ ___ ___ ___ ___ ___ ___ ___ ___

3 ___ ___ ___ ___ ___ ___ ___ ___ ___ ___ ___ ___ ___ ___ ___

4 ___ ___ ___ ___ ___ ___ ___ ___ ___

5 ___ ___ ___ ___ ___ ___ ___ ___ ___ ___

6 ___ ___ ___ ___ ___ ___ ___ ___ ___

7 ___ ___ ___ ___ ___

8 ___ ___ ___ ___ ___

9 ___ ___ ___

10 ___ ___ ___ ___ ___ ___ ___

canal	gin	interchangeable	railroads	steam
factory	Industrial	machinery	power	telegraph

1. ________________ was used to run engines on boats.
2. The ________________ sent dots and dashes long distances over wires.
3. ________________ parts allowed manufactured goods to be made and repaired more easily.
4. Factories in the Northeast began using ________________ to make cotton cloth.
5. During the ________________ Revolution, businesses changed to making goods on machines in factories.
6. ________________ took people and goods further, faster, and cheaper than canals.
7. ________________ boats were pulled by mules.
8. First water and then steam was used to ________________ machines.
9. Because of the cotton ________________, Southern farmers were growing more cotton.
10. In a ________________, many workers used machines to make goods.

The mystery word tells what all these sentences have in common. They are all about new

____

NAME:

UNIT 2 • ACTIVITY 26
Moving West

Many people moved west to find new homes. They often had an exciting trip. Read the paragraphs below. Use the words listed in the box to fill in the blanks. The paragraphs tell about some problems people had on a trip west.

float	barrels	deserts	goods	guide
mountains	oxen	trading posts	illness	covered wagon

Many settlers moved west in a(n) **1.** __________________. They tried to travel with a(n) **2.** __________________ who showed them the way. Very few of these settlers expected so many problems along the way.

Many settlers bought their supplies before they left Missouri. They had to buy **3.** __________________ of flour. It had to last them months. They had limited space on the wagon. They used **4.** __________________ to pull the heavy wagon.

First, they traveled across the plains. Then they had to go up and down the **5.** __________________. They also had to cross hot, dry **6.** __________________. There were very few **7.** __________________ along the way where they could get supplies.

During the trip, many people died from **8.** __________________. Broken wheels and tired animals forced people to leave many of their **9.** __________________ along the trail. They even had to use the wagon as a raft to **10.** __________________ across flooded streams. It was a very hard trip west. After they arrived, they built farms in the western wilderness.

UNIT 2 • ACTIVITY 27
Texas and the Mexican War

Write two sentences about each event on the time line. Write about who, what, where, and why. Find facts and details to use in your sentences. Use your textbook, the Internet, or another reference for information.

March 2, 1836 — Texas declares independence. ________________

March 6, 1836 — Alamo fighting ends. ________________

April 21, 1836 — Battle of San Jacinto is fought. ________________

December, 1845 — Texas becomes a state. ________________

March, 1846 — General Zachary Taylor advances to the Rio Grande River. ________________

May 13, 1846 — The United States declares war on Mexico. ________________

June 14, 1846 — Republic of California flag flown. ________________

September 14, 1847 — American troops capture Mexico City. ________________

February, 1848 — Treaty of Guadalupe Hidalgo signed. ________________

1853 — Gadsden Purchase made. ________________

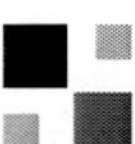

NAME:

UNIT 2 • ACTIVITY 28
Life in a Mining Town

Life in a western mining town was different from life in any other place in America. These towns grew quickly when gold or silver was discovered. Many disappeared when no more gold or silver was left.

Find out about life in these exciting towns. Next, answer these questions about mining towns. Then, in the space below, write a section of a newspaper to show life in a mining town. You might write a news article. You might create ads for goods or businesses. You might write letters to the editor about important issues. In anything you write, you should help your reader understand life in a mining town.

1. Who lived in mining towns? ______________________

2. Why did people move to mining towns? ______________________

3. What jobs did they do? ______________________

4. Where did people live, shop, eat, and work? ______________________

5. Did most people stay or leave town? Why? ______________________

6. How were mining towns different from other small towns? ______________________

NAME:

UNIT 2 • ACTIVITY 29
Changes in the West

Many changes happened when settlers began moving west. Below are eight cause-and-effect charts. Use a group listed in the box below to complete each cause. (One group is used more than once.) In the effect boxes, write the effect that resulted from each cause.

American Indians	farmers	the U. S. government
Indian agents	white hunters	

	Cause		Effect
1.	When ____________ killed millions of buffalo,	→	
2.	When ____________ attacked settlers,	→	
3.	When ____________ made the reservations smaller,	→	
4.	When ____________ sold rotten food at reservation stores,	→	
5.	When ____________ refused to live on the reservations,	→	
6.	When ____________ were forced onto reservations far from their homelands,	→	
7.	When ____________ began settling on the plains,	→	
8.	When ____________ leaders were captured by the army,	→	

NAME:

UNIT 2 • ACTIVITY 30
The Transcontinental Railroad

Complete each sentence using a word listed in the box. Write the words in the puzzle.

brake	Central	grants	Pacific	manufactured
Chinese	time	track	tunnel	Promontory

Across

2. The two railroad lines met in ___________, Utah.
6. The two companies built over 1700 miles of railroad ___________.
7. The ___________ Pacific started building its line from Sacramento, California.
8. Many ___________ workers built the western part of the railroad.
9. Many times a ___________ was blasted through a mountain instead of going over it.

Down

1. The railroad companies received land ___________ from Congress.
2. The Union ___________ Company helped build the transcontinental railroad.
3. Companies sent ___________ goods across the country faster and for less money.
4. Because railroads had a schedule to keep, everyone began using standard ___________.
5. An important safety invention for railroads was the air ___________.

NAME:

UNIT 2 • ACTIVITY 31
Westward Expansion

This map shows the westward expansion of the United States. It shows when each section of land was added. Use the map and what you know about westward expansion to answer the questions.

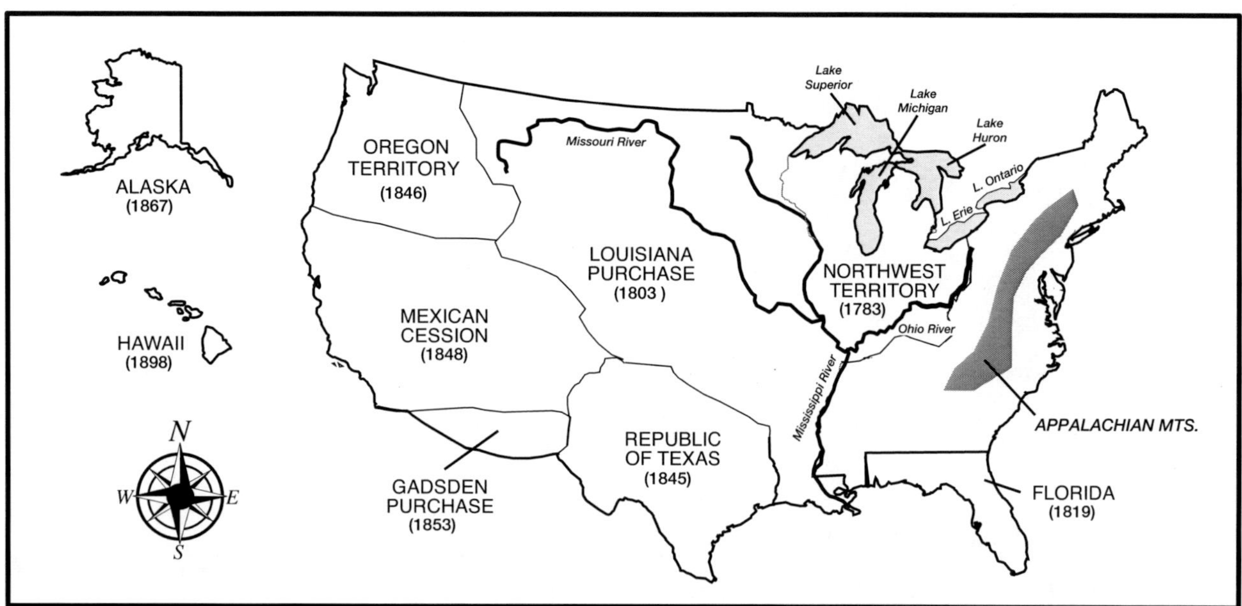

1. What was the first section of land added to the new United States? ____________________
2. In which section of land were the British encouraging American Indians to fight American settlers? ____________________
3. Which section was bought by Thomas Jefferson from the French government?
____
4. Which section was an independent country before it became a state?
____
5. Which section was purchased from Spain? ____________________
6. Which section became part of the United States at the end of the Mexican War?
____
7. Which section became part of the United States because of a treaty with Great Britain?
____
8. Which section was purchased from Mexico? ____________________
9. Which section was the last to become part of the United States? ____________________
10. How does this map illustrate Manifest Destiny? ____________________

____

NAME:

UNIT 2 • ACTIVITY 32
Differences Between the North and South

Before the Civil War, each part of the country had a different economy. They fit together. They were interdependent. One part depended on the other. One might have resources. It would trade those to the other for manufactured goods.

Each detail below tells about one part of the country. Write each in the chart under the part it describes.

Details

Many factories manufactured goods.

Most farmers grew cotton.

Shipping businesses moved goods back and forth across the ocean.

Ships left carrying mostly agricultural goods.

Recent immigrants lived in cities.

Railroads and canals connected much of the region.

Large plantations depended on slave labor.

Large banks loaned money to improve businesses.

Northern economy	Southern economy

NAME: ____________________

UNIT 2 • ACTIVITY 33
Civil War Issues

Americans disagreed about several issues before the Civil War. These disagreements led to the war. The three main issues were: slavery, sovereignty (supreme power), and trade laws. Read each sentence below. On the first line, write the issue it is about. On the second line, write which part of the country supported that statement. Then answer the last three questions.

1. Congress passed a tariff to protect American industries. ____________________

   ____

2. States should be able to nullify certain federal laws. ____________________

   ____

3. The states should not be able to choose which laws they want to obey.

   ____________________ ____________________

4. Slavery should continue. ____________________ ____________________

5. No person should own another person. ____________________ ____________________

6. People should be able to buy the cheapest goods no matter where they are made.

   ____________________ ____________________

7. No state should be able to leave and form its own country. ____________________

   ____

8. What stand did most Northerners take on these three issues? ____________________

   ____

9. What stand did most Southerners take on these three issues? ____________________

   ____

10. What issue did Abraham Lincoln warn could cause a war? ____________________

    ____

NAME:

UNIT 2 • ACTIVITY 34
Against Slavery

Many people, especially in the North, were against slavery. Some were abolitionists who wanted slavery to end immediately. Most were willing to go to war. Others were against slavery but did not want to split the country.

Each person listed in the box below fought against slavery. Choose one. Research his or her life using your textbook, the Internet, or other reference material. Find out what the person did to fight slavery. Fill in the chart with your notes about that person. Then present a short report to the class. While others present their reports, listen to the ideas, events, and opinions people had about slavery. Discuss the different actions people took against slavery.

Frederick Douglass	Sojourner Truth	Harriet Tubman
William Lloyd Garrison	Harriet Beecher Stowe	Angelina Grimke
Abraham Lincoln	John Brown	Wendell Phillips

Person	
Life	
Beliefs	
Actions against slavery	
Writings against slavery (if any)	

NAME:

UNIT 2 • ACTIVITY 35
Advantages and Disadvantages

Both the North and the South had advantages when the Civil War began. They also had disadvantages. Read each sentence below. Write whether the fact was about the North or the South. Then complete the sentence. Use facts and details to support your choice. Find these facts and details in your text or another source.

1. An advantage of the __________________ was it had a bigger population because __________

____.

2. An advantage of the __________________ was it had the best military leaders because _______

____.

3. An advantage of the __________________ was it had more money because _________________

____.

4. An advantage of the __________________ was it had more manufactured goods because _____

____.

5. An advantage of the __________________ was that it was defending its own land because _____

____.

6. An advantage of the __________________ was it had better transportation because _________

____.

7. A disadvantage of the __________________ was it lost many of the best military leaders because ____.

8. A disadvantage of the __________________ was it imported most of its goods because

____.

9. A disadvantage of the __________________ was it had had few railroads because

____.

10. A disadvantage of the __________________ was its economy depended on one export because

____.

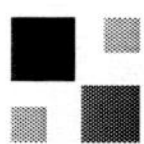

NAME:

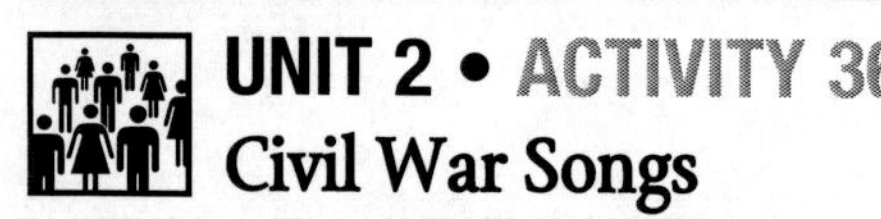

UNIT 2 • ACTIVITY 36
Civil War Songs

Many songs were written at the time of the Civil War. Some were sad. Some were marching or battle songs. Some were about the issues.

Using the Internet or another reference, find the words to a Civil War song. Read the words carefully. Answer the questions below about your song. Present the words to the class. You might sing them, recite them, or play a recording of the song. Discuss the different types of songs that your class finds.

1. What is the name of the song? ______________________________

2. Is it a religious song? ______________

3. What is the purpose of the song? Is it a marching song? Does it tell a story or try to change people's minds? ______________________________

4. Which side would have sung the song? ______________

5. Does it describe an event or use symbols? What are they? ______________

6. What are the most descriptive words in the song? ______________

7. Is it just about the Civil War or could it be sung about other times and events? ______________
____

8. What do you like best about the words to the song? ______________

9. What feelings do reading or listening to the song create? ______________

10. What is your opinion of how well this song accomplished its purpose? ______________
____

NAME:

UNIT 2 • ACTIVITY 37
Civil War Battles

Read about these battles of the Civil War. Locate where each one took place. Place the letter of the battle on the map where it took place. Then answer the questions.

a. Bull Run	**c.** New Orleans	**e.** Vicksburg	**g.** Gettysburg	**i.** Appomattox
b. Antietam	**d.** Shiloh	**f.** Richmond	**h.** Atlanta	

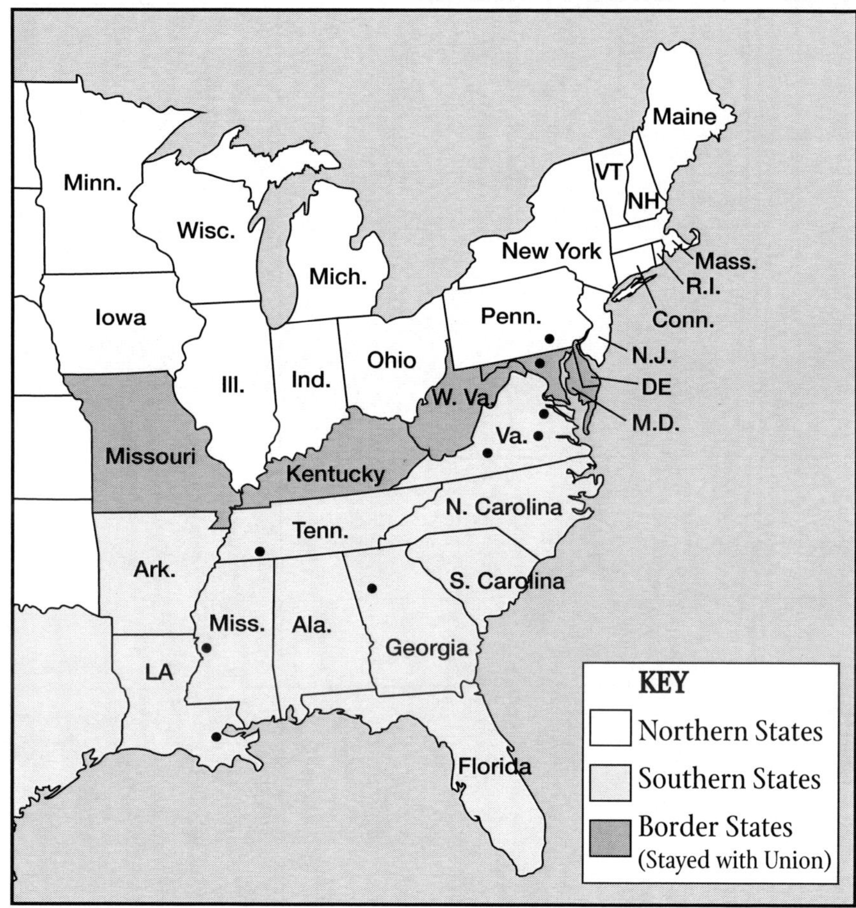

1. In what part of the country were most of the Civil War battles fought? ____________________

2. What part of the country felt it was defending its land? ____________________

3. What part of the country did not have a lot of damage? ____________________

4. How did the land and people change when battles were fought nearby? ____________________

____

5. Predict which side recovered from the war faster. Give one good reason to support your prediction. ____________________ ____________________

NAME:

UNIT 2 • ACTIVITY 38
Changes After the Civil War

The Civil War changed life for many Americans. Read and take notes on the ways life changed in the North and the South. Note the changes that happened for each topic in the chart. On another sheet of paper, use your notes to write two paragraphs. Compare and contrast how the Civil War affected life in the North and in the South.

	North	South
Factories		
Exports		
Farms and plantations		
Transportation		
Cities		
Workers		

NAME:

UNIT 2 • ACTIVITY 39
Reconstruction Changes Life

The following statements tell of life in the South before the Civil War. Work with a small group. For each statement, write a related sentence that tells about life in the South during Reconstruction. Then, with your group, plan a way to show before and after for one of these statements. You might do this with pictures, stories, letters, or skits.

1. Before the Civil War, most farmers grew cotton to sell. During Reconstruction, ______________________________.

2. Before the Civil War, large plantations used slaves as workers. During Reconstruction, ______________________________.

3. Before the Civil War, important plantation owners were elected to local, state, and national office. During Reconstruction, ______________________________.

4. Before the Civil War, many farmers owned small farms. During Reconstruction, ______________________________.

5. Before the Civil War, most slaves had no education or political power. During Reconstruction, ______________________________.

6. Before the Civil War, slaves did not own land. During Reconstruction, ______________________________.

In the space below, brainstorm ideas for your presentation.

NAME:

UNIT 2 • ACTIVITY 40
Reconstruction

Read the paragraphs below. Fill in each blank with the correct word listed in the box.

Emancipation Proclamation	North	vote	black codes
Thirteenth Amendment	South	Confederate	assassinated
Freedman's Bureau	Johnson	Congress	Reconstruction

The Civil War was fought between the **1.** ____________________ and the **2.** ____________________. Then the **3.** ____________________ General Robert E. Lee surrendered. This ended the Civil War. Soon after, President Lincoln was **4.** ____________________.

During the Civil War, President Lincoln issued the **5.** ____________________. This freed slaves in Southern states. The **6.** ____________________ abolished slavery everywhere in the United States.

Much of the South had been destroyed by the fighting. Transportation, farms, and the government had to be rebuilt. President **7.** ____________________ was not able to control Congress. Congress began using its own **8.** ____________________ plans.

Southern states passed the **9.** ____________________. These limited the rights of African Americans. This upset the Radical Republicans in **10.** ____________________. They passed Constitutional amendments. These protected the rights of African Americans. This included the right to **11.** ____________________. Congress also set up the **12.** ____________________. This department helped former slaves improve their lives.

NAME:

UNIT 3 • ACTIVITY 41
Technology Changes

Use the words listed in the box and the clues below to complete the puzzle.

industrial	factory	mass	steam	engine
mill	raw	technology	urban	machines

Across

5. the use of scientific knowledge in trade and industry
6. having to do with cities
7. When things are made in large amounts for less money, they are ________________ produced.
8. materials in their natural state
9. an energy source used to run engines

Down

1. a building where goods are made in large amounts, usually by machine
2. items with fixed and moving parts used for doing work
3. a machine that makes something move or run
4. having to do with business, trade, or manufacturing
7. a factory that produces goods, especially cloth or flour

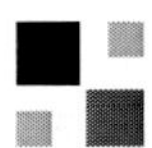

NAME:

UNIT 3 • ACTIVITY 42
The Industrial Revolution

Read each set of statements. Then put the events in order. For each set, write a 1 next to the event that happened first. Write a 2 next to the event that happened second. Write a 3 next to what happened last.

Set 1

_______ Water is used to power machines.

_______ Electricity is used to power machines.

_______ Steam is used to power machines.

Set 2

_______ Workers watch as computers control looms.

_______ Workers weave cloth on power looms in factories.

_______ Workers weave cloth on hand looms in their homes.

Set 3

_______ American factories spin thread and weave cloth.

_______ Manufactured goods use parts made in many different countries.

_______ English industries use factories and machines.

Set 4

_______ Gun factories put together guns from interchangeable parts.

_______ Most goods are made from interchangeable parts.

_______ Gunsmiths make one gun at a time by hand.

NAME:

UNIT 3 • ACTIVITY 43
Effects of the Industrial Revolution

In the mid-1800s, mass production and industrialization changed life for many Americans. Choose one person or group described below. Create before and after pictures for that person or group. In one, show what life was like before industrialization. In the other, show how the life or activities of this person or group changed with industrialization.

1. Jane grew up on a farm. She moved to Lowell, Massachusetts. She worked in the mills. Show how her life changed.
2. Jason had a small store in a town in Connecticut. A large factory was built in the town. Many workers moved to town to work in the factory. Show how Jason's business changed.
3. The Winston family owned a farm in Ohio. They bought several new farming machines. Show how life on the Winstons' farm changed.
4. Thomas lived near Rochester, New York. The Erie Canal was built nearby. Soon large factories were also built nearby. They shipped their goods on the canal and later on the railroads. Show how the area where Thomas lived changed.
5. Matthew worked in a furniture factory. It took him a week to make a table. Then the factory owner changed to making tables with interchangeable parts. Show how his job changed.
6. The Billings Flour Mills were in Chicago. They ground wheat into flour. Show how changes in transportation improved their business.

Before	After

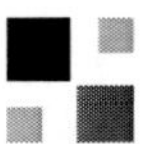

NAME:

UNIT 3 • ACTIVITY 44
Urbanization

In the 1800s, many American cities grew and changed. Those changes affected the people who lived there. Answer the following questions in complete sentences. You will need to think about the question. You may need to research *urbanization* in reference material or on the Internet.

1. What caused towns to quickly grow into cities? ______________________________
____.

2. How did growing factories and cities affect farmers? ______________________________
____.

3. How did a city change when many people moved to it? ______________________________
____.

4. What made the life of factory workers so hard? ______________________________
____.

5. How did growing cities and factories affect people's health? ______________________________
____.

6. How did urban transportation affect where people lived and worked? ______________________________
____.

7. How did growing cities affect the land and water near it? ______________________________
____.

8. Why did people want to live in the suburbs instead of in the cities? ______________________________
____.

9. How was life different for people living in a small town than for those living in an industrial city? ______________________________
____.

10. Would you have liked to live in an industrial city at this time? Support your opinion with facts about cities. ______________________________
____.

NAME:

UNIT 3 • ACTIVITY 45
Tenement Apartments

Read this description of a tenement apartment. People would have lived in it after 1860. Then complete the sentences. Some will ask you what you think. Use the facts to make a good opinion.

Tenements were apartment buildings. In New York City, many were built after 1860. They were built so that immigrants would have a cheap place to live. Often, seven or more people lived in one apartment.

Each apartment had three rooms. The largest room was the front room. It was the only room with a window for air or light. Behind it was the kitchen and bedroom. Each kitchen had a wood or coal fireplace. Some people brought their own coal cookstove. Tenements did not have bathrooms or running water. The toilets were in the backyard. The garbage went into a box in front of the building. The building had no electricity. The halls and stairs were dark.

1. A tenement had these three rooms: ______________________________.
2. Because there were so many people, I think some slept ______________________.
3. Families cooked on ______________________________.
4. Tenement apartments did not have ______________________________.
5. One problem getting to a fifth-floor apartment was ______________________.
6. If there were four apartments on a floor, there might be __________________ people living there.
7. Tenement apartments smelled bad because ______________________________.
8. I think tenement apartments were dangerous because ______________________.
9. I would not have liked living in a tenement apartment because __________________.
10. I think laws should have improved the tenements by ______________________.

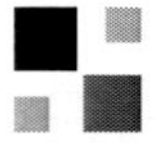

NAME:

UNIT 3 • ACTIVITY 46
Reformers

Many reformers wanted to help workers. They wanted to improve working conditions. Research the working conditions in factories around 1900. Research facts from newspapers, photographs, reports, and letters. Take notes about these topics. Add facts to the chart that you feel are important.

On another sheet of paper, write a report to the government. Describe your findings. Also, suggest how the government could improve working conditions. This list might include new laws, rules, or inspections. Share your report with your class.

	Factory conditions
Workers	
Hours	
Pay	
Factory safety	
Factory cleanliness	

UNIT 3 • ACTIVITY 47
Technology Improves Life

People's lives changed because of new technology. It changed what they did at home and at the office. They were able to do things faster and more safely.

Below is a list of some new inventions after 1865. Read each riddle. Choose an invention listed in the box to answer the riddle. Then write a riddle of your own for another invention. You will not use all the inventions that are listed.

bicycle	elevator	electric lightbulb	sewing machine
subway	telephone	typewriter	washing machine

1. I was built in Boston but was soon in New York City, too. First trolley cars used me and then trains. The streets were safer because I was underground. I am a(n) ______________________.

2. Alexander Graham Bell made me. He took me to the Centennial Exhibition. People did not believe I worked. Then they listened to me. Families and businesses still use me. I am a(n) ______________________.

3. People made many different versions of me. Early ones had wooden wheels. Some had huge front tires. Many people rode me to have fun when the sun was out. I am a(n) ______________________.

4. I was at the Centennial Exhibition. No one paid much attention to me. I was slow because I used two keyboards. When these were combined, I became faster than handwriting. I am a(n) ______________________.

5. Your riddle: ____

____

____

____

NAME:

UNIT 3 • ACTIVITY 48
Reform Groups

During the early 1900s, many reform groups wanted to change American life. Each group wanted to change something different. People sometimes belonged to more than one group. Each group worked very hard for the change it wanted.

In the box below is a list of reform groups. Choose one. Read about it. Learn what the people believed and what they did. Answer the questions below to understand the group. Then write a letter to the editor. Tell whether you support the ideas of this reform group. Tell whether you agree with the actions they are taking. Use an additional sheet of paper, if necessary.

women's suffrage	temperance	monopolies and trusts
public education	child labor	railroad regulation

Group chosen: ______________________________

1. WHO: Who was important in this group? ______________________________
2. WHAT: What did this group believe was wrong? ______________________________
3. WHY: Why did this group want change to happen? ______________________________
4. WHEN: When was the group active? ______________________________
5. WHERE: Where did this group take action? ______________________________
6. HOW: How did this group work to create change? ______________________________
7. WHAT: What was the result of this group and its actions? ______________________________

Letter to the Editor: ______________________________

____

____

____

____

____

NAME:

UNIT 3 • ACTIVITY 49
Coming to America

Immigrants came to America for many reasons. Some reasons are listed in the box below. Read each sentence. Write the reason why each speaker came to America.

religious	economic	political	adventure

1. "All of my friends were arrested. We had been talking about the king's plans. None of us agreed with them." ________________
2. "My brother will get my father's farm. There is no good land nearby for me to buy." ________________
3. "Since all the potatoes rotted, there is no food for my family to eat." ________________
4. "Soldiers are attacking us because we are Jewish." ________________
5. "I want to go west, see Indians, find gold, and own a cattle ranch." ________________
6. "My family has very little. I want to earn enough to send them money every month." ________________
7. "I know I am lucky. I will find gold when I get to California." ________________
8. "If we do not do what the church says, no one sells us food." ________________
9. "Everyone is taking sides. They are fighting about independence. I just want to live quietly with my family." ________________
10. "In America, it does not matter if I am an orphan. I can still earn money and become a powerful businessman." ________________

Imagine that you are an immigrant who said one of the sentences above. Write a journal entry about why you left your homeland. Use details to tell why you came to America. Use another sheet of paper, if needed.

____

____

____

____

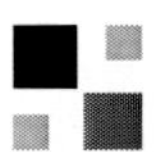

NAME:

UNIT 3 • ACTIVITY 50
Local Immigration

Use reference material or the Internet to find out about the immigrants that settled in one community. You might choose your community. You might choose one nearby or in another state. Answer these questions about that community. Then, on another sheet of paper, write a short history of immigrants in this community. Draw or locate pictures to illustrate what happened.

Community: ______________________

1. From what countries did most of the immigrants come? ______________________

____

2. When did they move to this community? ______________________

3. Did different immigrant groups come at different times? If so, tell in what order they came.

____

4. Why did most of the immigrants leave their homeland? ______________________

____

5. Where did they live when they first arrived? ______________________

6. What jobs did many of them take when they first arrived? ______________________

____

Did different immigrant groups take different jobs? If so, what were they? ______________________

____

7. What parts of their culture were part of their life in America? ______________________

____

8. What is seen in this community today that came from their culture? ______________________

____

9. How did individual immigrants contribute to the community? ______________________

____

10. Where are recent immigrants to this community coming from? ______________________

____

NAME: ________________________________

UNIT 3 • ACTIVITY 51
Changes in Immigration

This chart tells how many immigrants arrived in this country in certain years. It lists only a few countries. It tells how many immigrants came from that country that year. Use the facts in this chart to answer the questions below.

	Great Britain	Ireland	Russia and nearby countries	Italy	China
1830	1,153	2,721	3	9	0
1850	51,085	164,004	31	431	3
1870	103,677	56,996	907	1,382	15,740
1890	69,730	53,024	35,598	52,003	1,716
1910	68,941	29,855	186,792	215,537	1,968
1930	31,000	23,445	2,772	22,327	1,589

1. In what year did the most Chinese come to America? ____________________
2. From what country did the most immigrants arrive in 1850? ____________________
3. What year and from what country did the most immigrants come? ____________________
4. From what country did the fewest immigrants come? ____________________
5. Did most Irish come before or after most Italians? ____________________
6. In what year did the fewest total immigrants come to America? ____________________
7. Compare and contrast immigration from Russia and the region around it in 1890, 1910, and 1930. ____
8. How many immigrants came in 1850? ____________________ From which country did most of them come? ____________________
9. How many immigrants came in 1910? ____________________ From which country did most of them come? ____________________
10. Write a sentence to compare immigration in 1850 with that in 1910. ____________________

____

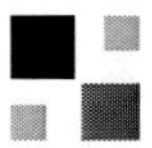

NAME:

UNIT 3 • ACTIVITY 52
Immigration Puzzle

Many immigrants entered the United States at New York City. Others entered at San Francisco, California. Millions of immigrants also came into other cities. Use a word listed in the box to complete the sentences. Write each word in the puzzle. Then use the mystery word in the last sentence.

1 ___ ___ ___ [___] ___

2 ___ ___ ___ [___] ___ ___ ___ ___ ___ ___ ___

3 ___ ___ [___] ___ ___ ___

4 ___ ___ [___] ___

5 ___ ___ [___] ___ ___

6 ___ ___ [___] ___ ___ ___

7 ___ ___ ___ [___] ___

8 ___ ___ ___ [___] ___ ___ ___

9 ___ ___ ___ [___] ___ ___ ___

10 ___ ___ ___ ___ ___ [___] ___ ___ ___

afraid	Angel	Chinese	Eastern	Ellis
examination	Exclusion	family	speak	ship

1. In New York, many people first entered the United States at ____________________ Island.
2. Every immigrant had to go through a(n) ____________________.
3. Sometimes a(n) ____________________ was sent back because they were unhealthy.
4. In 1900, most immigrants came to America on a(n) ____________________.
5. In San Francisco, many Chinese immigrants spent months on ____________________ Island before entering the United States.
6. Most immigrants were ____________________ they would not be allowed into America.
7. Many immigrants were confused because they did not ____________________ English.
8. Many ____________________ immigrants came to work on the railroads.
9. Many immigrants from ____________________ Europe came around 1900.
10. The Chinese ____________________ Act of 1882 ended most Chinese immigration.

Mystery Word: Use the outlined word in the puzzle to complete this sentence:

Millions of people were ____________________ to America in the late 1800s.

NAME:

UNIT 3 • ACTIVITY 53
Naturalization Test

Many immigrants come to the United States. Not all of them become citizens. Only citizens can vote. The process to become a citizen is called naturalization. To become a naturalized citizen, you must understand, speak, and write English. You must also pass a test. It is about U. S. history and U.S. government. Here are a few questions similar to those on a naturalization test. Fill in the circle of your answer.

1. What is the legislative branch of the federal government called?
- ○ Congress
- ○ the Supreme Court
- ○ the presidency
- ○ the House of Representatives

2. What is the head executive of a city government called?
- ○ governor
- ○ mayor
- ○ city president
- ○ senator

3. Which president freed the slaves?
- ○ Thomas Jefferson
- ○ Abraham Lincoln
- ○ George Washington
- ○ John F. Kennedy

4. In what year was the Constitution written?
- ○ 1621
- ○ 1787
- ○ 1860
- ○ 1950

5. What is the minimum voting age in the United States?
- ○ 18
- ○ 21
- ○ 30
- ○ 25

6. Who becomes president if the president and vice president should die?
- ○ the Mayor of Washington, D. C.
- ○ the Speaker of the House of Representatives
- ○ the Majority Leader of the Senate
- ○ the Chief Justice of the Supreme Court

NAME:

UNIT 3 • ACTIVITY 54
Understanding Foreign Policy

Sometimes acting out an idea helps you to understand it better. Discuss each term with a small group. The terms are all about foreign policy. Create a skit to show an example of each word. Use the information in the chart to prepare your skit. Present your skits to the class. Have your classmates guess which word your actions are illustrating.

Foreign Policy terms	Definition	Ideas to act out
Isolationism		
Neutrality		
Trade		
Alliance		
Internationalism		

NAME:

UNIT 3 • ACTIVITY 55
What Policy Is This?

Match each word with its meaning. Write the letter of the definition on the line.

Words	Meanings
1. _______ neutral	**a.** the way nations deal with other nations
2. _______ alliance	**b.** a policy of being actively involved with other countries in the world
3. _______ isolation	**c.** an agreement among nations
4. _______ foreign policy	**d.** a policy of remaining separate from the affairs of other countries
5. _______ internationalism or globalization	**e.** a policy of not taking sides in a disagreement

Use each term in a sentence that gives an example about the United States.

6. neutral ____

____

7. alliance ____

____

8. isolation ____

____

9. foreign policy ____

____

10. internationalism or globalization ______________________________

____

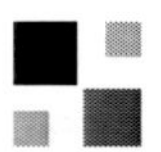

NAME:

UNIT 3 • ACTIVITY 56
What in the World Happened?

Read these events from U. S. history. Decide which type of foreign policy is being used. Complete the sentences using the correct foreign policy listed in the box.

neutrality	internationalism	isolationism	imperialism

1. George Washington did not take sides in the European war. He followed a policy of ______________________.

2. The United States took control of the Philippines from Spain. This was a policy of ______________________.

3. Woodrow Wilson tried to keep the United States out of World War I. He wanted to keep America separate from the war. He followed a policy of ______________________

4. Congress voted not to join the League of Nations. It wanted to follow a foreign policy of ______________________.

5. During the Great Depression, many countries followed the same foreign policy. They concentrated on problems within their country. They followed a policy of ______________________.

6. The United States helped win World War II. It supported the Allies with materials, money, and its military. The United States followed a foreign policy of ______________________.

7. After World War II, the United States became a leader in world affairs. It was involved in countries all over the world. It followed a policy of ______________________.

8. During the Cold War, the United States took action against communists. These actions were all over the world. It followed a policy of ______________________.

NAME:

UNIT 4 • ACTIVITY 57
American Imperialism

Look at a world map. Read the statements below about American imperialism. On the lines, write the country that is involved. The countries are listed in the box.

Panama	China	Hawaii	the Dominican Republic
Philippines	Guam	Cuba	Puerto Rico

1. The Open Door Policy opened trade with ________________________.
2. Spain controlled ________________________. Then it became an American territory. Its people have voted not to become a state.
3. ________________________ became an independent country after the Spanish-American War. The United States could still interfere in its affairs.
4. After the Spanish-American War, the ________________________ wanted its freedom. It fought the United States for many years. It did not become independent until 1933.
5. The United States helped ________________________ win its independence from Colombia. Then the United States rented land there. It built a canal on that land.
6. After the Spanish-American War, the United States took the small island of ________________________. It became important to ships crossing the Pacific Ocean. It is still an American territory.
7. ________________________ became a United States territory in 1898. In 1959, it became a state.
8. ________________________ had a lot of debts. In 1905, President Theodore Roosevelt took charge of its finances.

NAME:

UNIT 4 • ACTIVITY 58
Farm Life

American farmers were having many problems. Match the problem below to its cause. Write the letter of the correct cause on the line.

Problems

1. _______ Crop prices were low.
2. _______ Transportation prices were high.
3. _______ Farmers had many debts.
4. _______ Farmers had little political power.
5. _______ Farmers were losing their farms.

Causes

a. Railroads had a monopoly.

b. Rich businessmen were elected to state legislatures.

c. New machines made farms more productive.

d. Farmers could not pay back bank loans.

e. Farmers had to buy expensive machines, and they paid high transportation costs and high interest rates.

Match the problem below to a suggested solution. Write the correct letter of the solution on the line.

Problems

6. _______ Politicians were controlled by big business.
7. _______ Farmers paid a lot of taxes, but rich people paid very little.
8. _______ Transportation costs were high.
9. _______ Crop prices were low.
10. _______ No one listened to farmers' ideas.

Solutions

a. regulation of prices

b. publicly owned railroads

c. income tax

d. Granges and Alliances

e. popular election of senators

Answer this question in a complete sentence.

11. Which suggested solutions became part of American life?_______________

____

NAME:

UNIT 4 • ACTIVITY 59
The Biggest Businesses

Around 1900, big business was causing problems for many Americans. Use words from the box to fill in the blanks in the sentences below. You may have to research some of the people or terms that relate to big business.

Andrew Carnegie	Theodore Roosevelt	railroad	monopoly	regulate
Sherman Anti-Trust	high, fixed prices	Supreme Court	trustbuster	trust

1. ______________________ owned steel companies. His companies put others out of business. That gave him more business. His steel company became huge.

A **2.** ______________________ is when one company controls all goods or services. It has no competition. Only one railroad came near many farms. These farmers had to pay **3.** ______________________ to ship their crops. They had no choice.

A **4.** ______________________ is when a few huge companies control one type of goods or services. Standard Oil was part of one. Everyone in the oil industry worked together to keep the price of oil high. John D. Rockefeller owned this company. He controlled this powerful industry.

Congress passed the **5.** ______________________ Act to control big business. The **6.** ______________________ said that the government could not control manufacturing. The Act was not enforced. Then President **7.** ______________________ wanted to **8.** ______________________ big business. He enforced the act. He was called a **9.** ______________________. He forced the **10.** ______________________ industry to change.

Today, though, big businesses are even more powerful than in 1900.

NAME:

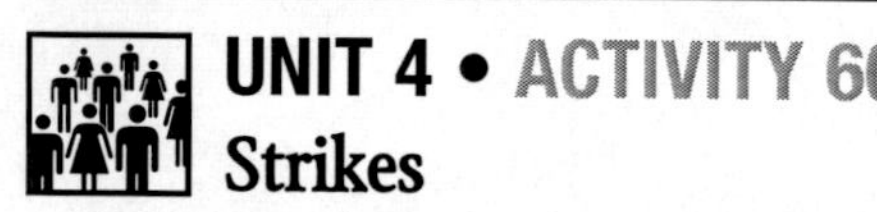

UNIT 4 • ACTIVITY 60
Strikes

American labor called many strikes between 1877 and 1910. Choose one of these strikes from the list in the box. Work with a partner. Find the answers to the questions about that strike. Then present the facts and opinions of each side to the class. Add your opinion of the issues and why you believe as you do.

Railroad Strike 1877	Pullman Strike 1894
Homestead Steel Strike 1892	1902 Coal Strike
Coeur d'Alene Miners Strike 1892	1909 Garment Workers Strike

1. What strike are you researching? ____________________
2. What companies were involved in the strike? ____________________
3. What jobs did the workers do? ____________________
4. What problems caused this strike? ____________________

   ____
5. Which labor union called the strike? ____________________
6. What did the company say about the strike and the workers? ____________________

   ____
7. What methods did the union use against the company? ____________________
8. What methods did the company use against the union? ____________________
9. How did the strike affect the company's business? ____________________

   ____
10. Did the local, state, or federal government get involved? If so, what did they do? ____________________

    ____
11. What was the outcome for the strikers? ____________________
12. What was the outcome for the company? ____________________

NAME:

UNIT 4 • ACTIVITY 61
World War I at Home

During World War I, the U. S. government printed posters. Each had a special message. They used the posters to encourage Americans to do certain things. Posters often used words or pictures as symbols. Look at this poster. Then answer the questions.

1. What pictures in the poster are symbols? ______________________________

____

2. What words in the poster are symbols? ______________________________

____

3. What does the poster want Americans to do? ______________________________

____

4. Does the poster tell people to send this food to someone? ______________________________

____

5. What will happen to the food that is not bought, if people eat less? ______________________________

____

6. How do you think people responded to the poster? ______________________________

____

NAME:

UNIT 4 • ACTIVITY 62
The Versailles Conference

The Versailles Conference was held at the end of World War I. Many important decisions were made there. Read about the conference. Then answer the questions below.

1. Who were the four leaders who made most of the decisions at the conference?

2. What did the U. S. leader want this conference to do?

3. Which country was forced to take the blame for the war?

4. What are reparations?

   Who had to pay them?

5. What was a protectorate?

6. From what countries was land taken to create modern-day Poland and Czechoslovakia?

7. What happened to Germany's colonies?

8. What happened to the Turkish Empire?

9. What was the purpose of the League of Nations?

10. How do you think Germany felt about the results of the conference? Support your opinion with two facts.

NAME:

UNIT 4 • ACTIVITY 63
Urban Life in the 1920s

American life had changed by the 1920s. People did and used many new things. Read about the 1920s in reference material or on the Internet. For each topic, find two examples of how life was changed. Then write about a person living in the 1920s. Include your facts about life at that time.

	Examples of how it changed life
New technology in the home	
Automobiles	
Commercial radio	
Prohibition	
Jazz	
Urbanization	

Life in the 1920s: ____

____

____

____

____

____

NAME: ____________________

UNIT 4 • ACTIVITY 64
Because It Was the Great Depression

Read each sentence. Think about life during the Great Depression. Think about what caused it. Complete each sentence. If you are not sure of an answer, read about the topic in reference material or on the Internet.

1. During the Great Depression, workers lost their jobs because ____________________

   ____________________.

2. People could not take their savings out of the bank because ____________________

   ____________________.

3. Unemployed workers could not get new jobs because ____________________

   ____________________.

4. Imported goods were more expensive because ____________________

   ____________________.

5. Families did not have enough to eat because ____________________

   ____________________.

6. Stores went out of business because ____________________

   ____________________.

7. Factories made fewer goods because ____________________

   ____________________.

8. People lost their homes because ____________________

   ____________________.

9. Families moved to California because ____________________

   ____________________.

10. Many people lost hope in the American dream because ____________________

    ____________________.

NAME:

UNIT 4 • ACTIVITY 65
The New Deal

The programs of the New Deal helped Americans. There were three kinds of programs.

Relief—immediate help from the government to those in need

Recovery—long-term help getting the economy back to normal

Reform—changes so that these problems would not happen again

The box below has a list of actions and programs. All were part of the New Deal. Write each one on the chart under the type of program that it was. Use the definitions above to help you choose. Be sure you know what the program did before you make your choice.

federal money to states to help people	WPA	Social Security
National Labor Relations Board	TVA	bank holiday
Federal Deposit Insurance Corporation	CCC	crop controls
Fair Labor Standards Act	minimum wage	

Relief	**Recovery**	**Reform**

NAME:

UNIT 4 • ACTIVITY 66
Making the Depression Worse

All of the United States suffered during the Great Depression. One part of the country suffered even more because of the weather. The farmers in these places had a very hard time. Read these sentences. Use a word listed in the box to complete them. The mystery word will tell you the name of the area.

1 ___ ___ ___ ___ ___ ___ ___

2 ___ ___ ___ ___ ___

3 ___ ___ ___ ___ ___ ___ ___ ___ ___ ___ ___ ___

4 ___ ___ ___ ___ ___ ___

___

5 ___ ___ ___ ___ ___

6 ___ ___ ___ ___ ___

7 ___ ___ ___ ___ ___

8 ___ ___ ___ ___ ___ ___

baked	crops	drought	grasshoppers
Plains	storms	under	winds

1. These states had a ____________________ because there was little rain.
2. The dust came in ____________________ the doors.
3. When the crops grew, the ____________________ ate them.
4. Huge dust ____________________ caused animals to die because they could not breathe.
5. The earth ____________________ in the hot, dry weather.
6. ____________________ shriveled and died from lack of water.
7. ____________________ blew away the dry topsoil.
8. These storms hit the Great ____________________.

Mystery words: Many people left the ____________________ ____________________ states.

NAME:

UNIT 4 • ACTIVITY 67
The Home Front

World War II changed life for everyone in the United States. Read the topics listed below about the World War II period. Read the sentences. For each group of sentences, write the topic described.

women in factories	migrant workers on farms	rationing
relocation camps	recycling drives	price controls
defense production	African Americans move north	
war bonds	Manhattan Project	

1. The military needed food, but farmers joined the army. Mexicans came north to work in the fields. They helped grow the crops. ______________________
2. The government limited many goods, such as meat and shoes. The military needed these goods. The government controlled the amount of these goods people at home could buy.

   ____
3. Factories stopped making household goods, such as washing machines. They switched to making planes, tanks, and other war supplies. ______________________
4. Factories needed workers. Rosie the Riveter was the symbol of these workers. They did much of the factory work. ______________________
5. The President gave an order. A company could not discriminate if it wanted to do business with the government. Because of this order, many African Americans found factory jobs. They improved their lives. ______________________
6. Many Japanese and Japanese Americans lived in America. During the war, they were forced to move. They were sent to guarded camps to live. ______________________
7. Most raw materials were used to make war goods. So, people collected newspapers and cans. Industry used these to make new consumer goods. ______________________
8. When there are not many goods, prices go up. The government did not want this to happen. They controlled prices so they would not go up. ______________________
9. The government needed money to pay for the war. Taxes were already high. People helped the government by buying these to save money. This supported the war.

   ____
10. During the war, the U.S. government did research. They were trying to develop an atomic bomb. They had people working in secret on this. ______________________

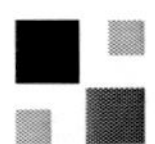

NAME:

UNIT 4 • ACTIVITY 68
World War II

Write the number of each of the events on the map near where they happened. Numbers may be used more than once if the event happened in different areas.

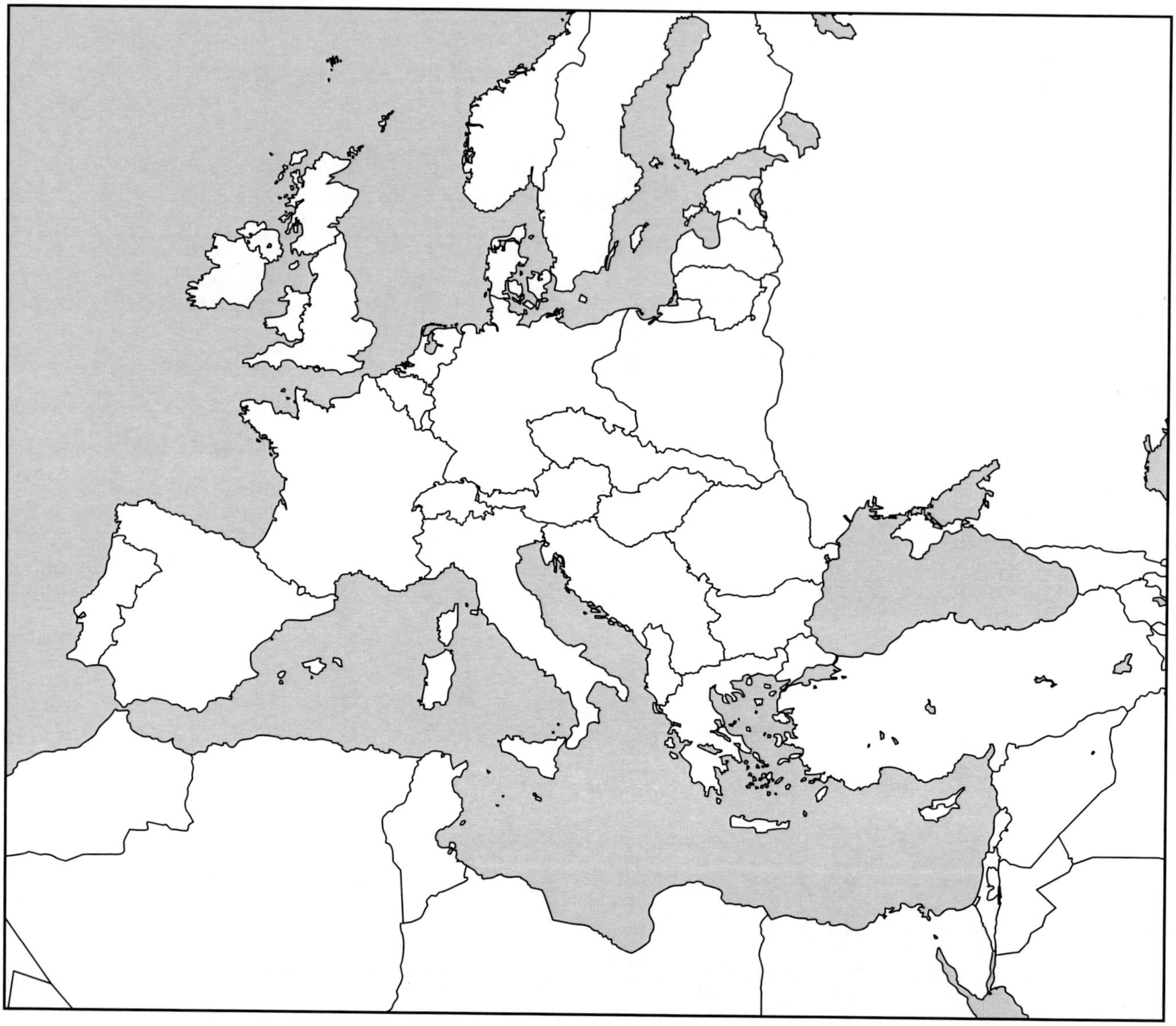

1. Germany invades Poland.
2. Soviet Union invades Baltic States.
3. Germany uses a Blitzkrieg war.
4. Germany bombs English cities.
5. Germany and Italy control much of North Africa.
6. Germany invades the Soviet Union.
7. Allies bomb German cities.
8. Allies invade North Africa.
9. Soviets push Germans back at Stalingrad.
10. Allied forces invade southern Italy.
11. D-Day as Allied forces invade northern France.
12. Soviets invade Poland.

NAME: ______________________________

UNIT 4 • ACTIVITY 69
Some Results of World War II

The world was not the same after World War II. It affected people everywhere. Complete the following sentences.

1. Much of Europe was in ruins. These countries ______________________________

______________________________.

2. The United States took control of Japan. The Americans ______________________________

______________________________.

3. A united Germany did not exist after the war. The Allies ______________________________

______________________________.

4. The Soviet Union was a communist country. It wanted ______________________________

______________________________.

5. The Soviet Union controlled countries in Eastern Europe. These countries ______________________________

______________________________.

6. America was the most powerful country in the world. Its economy ______________________________

______________________________.

7. Most American soldiers returned home. The government helped them by ______________________________

______________________________.

8. New technology was developed during the war. After the war, this technology was used to _____

______________________________.

9. Korea was divided because of political differences. This happened because one side __________

______________________________.

10. The United Nations was founded. Its goals include ______________________________

______________________________.

NAME:

UNIT 4 • ACTIVITY 70
The Cold War

After World War II, the Soviet Union was a communist dictatorship. The United States was a democratic country. They were the two most powerful countries in the world. They competed to see who would have the most influence in the world. Each wanted the most powerful military. They wanted the most missiles. They tried to stop each other from getting more influence. This time line shows Cold War events. Use it to answer the questions below.

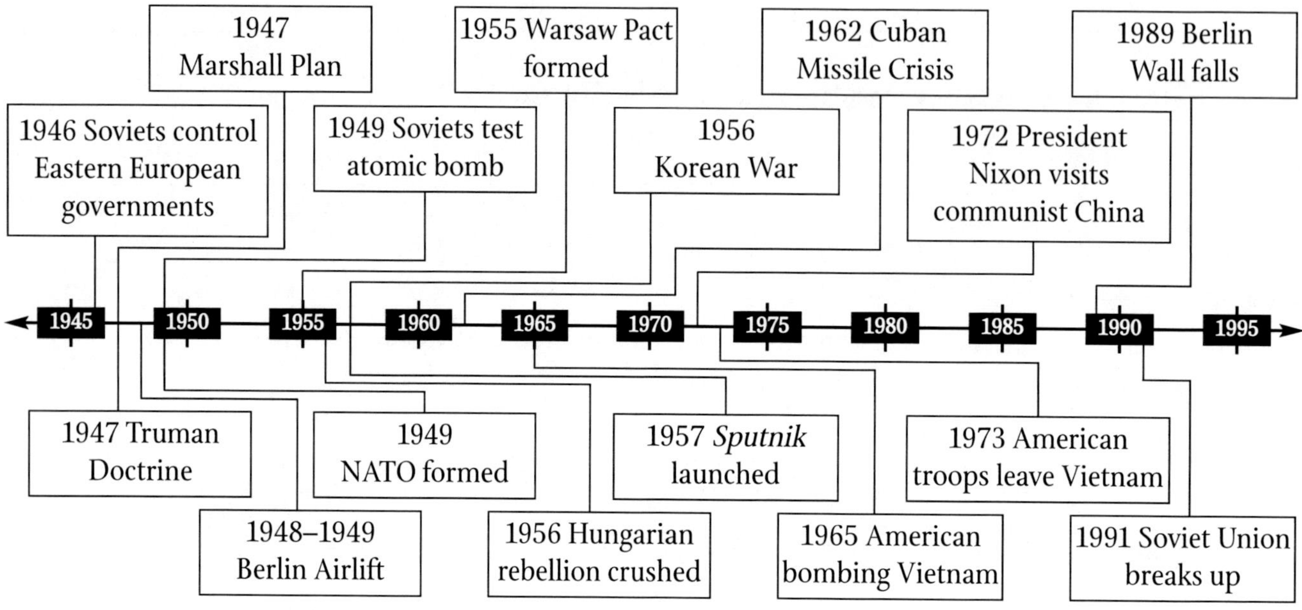

1. The United States wanted to stop communism from spreading. What were three events in which they tried to do this? ______________________________

____

2. What were two events that showed Soviet technology? ______________________________

____

3. What were two events that showed America's involvement with European countries? __________

____

4. What were two events that showed America's involvement with Asian countries? __________

____

5. What two alliances formed during the Cold War? ______________________________

____

6. Which event involved a threat close to the United States? ______________________________

____

7. What event happened in 1989? How did it symbolize the end of the Cold War? __________

____

8. What happened to the Soviet Union? ______________________________

____

NAME:

UNIT 4 • ACTIVITY 71
The Civil Rights Movement

This chart lists some important events in the Civil Rights Movement. Work with others to fill in the chart. Research each event. Describe the changes people wanted. Tell what happened at that event or as a result of that event. Then answer the questions below the chart.

Event	Changes people wanted	What happened?
1954—*Brown v. Board of Education of Topeka, Kansas*		
1955—Montgomery bus boycott		
1957—Little Rock school desegregation		
1960—Greensboro sit-ins		
1961—Freedom Riders		
1962—James Meredith enters the University of Alabama		
1963—March on Washington		
1964—Freedom Summer		
1965—Selma to Montgomery March		

1. Which of these events would you have liked to be part of? Why? ______________________

____

2. How did events like these change American life? ______________________

____

NAME:

UNIT 4 • ACTIVITY 72
After World War II

Life in America changed after World War II. Many more people moved into the middle class. Use the words listed in the box to complete the paragraph below about life in America after the war.

television set	consumer	G.I. Bill	schools	baby boom
veterans	interstate highway	credit card	shopping centers	suburbs

After the war, life changed. When **1.** ______________________ returned, many went to school, bought homes, and started businesses. The **2.** ______________________ helped them. Many moved to newly built houses. Most were in the **3.** ______________________. Many of these houses looked alike.

Americans had saved their money during the war. Now, they had money to spend. They bought many **4.** ______________________ goods, such as cars. They also bought a new kind of entertainment. Soon many homes had a(n) **5.** ______________________.

Americans began to travel more. The federal government planned a(n) **6.** ______________________ system. Its roads made crossing the country much easier.

After the war many couples had children. So many babies were born, it was called the **7.** ______________________. New **8.** ______________________ had to be built as these children became older.

Many Americans had good jobs. They had money to spend. They enjoyed shopping. A new way of paying for goods was created. With a(n) **9.** ______________________, people could spend now and pay later. In the suburbs, new **10.** ______________________ were built with many stores together. Life was much different from what it had been before the war.

NAME:

UNIT 4 • ACTIVITY 73
Youth of the 1960s

In the 1960s, many American youth rebelled. They rebelled against the life of their parents. Their music and art reflected their unhappiness. So did their actions and dress. Research the 1960s youth movement at the library, on the Internet, or with other resources.

Find examples of how young people expressed their anger, dreams, and unhappiness. Share one example with the class. You might analyze a song. You might show a photograph. You might read something written at that time.

Based on your presentation and those of your classmates, tell what these people believed and what they wanted to change. Tell how they expressed their ideas. Use the organizer below to take your notes.

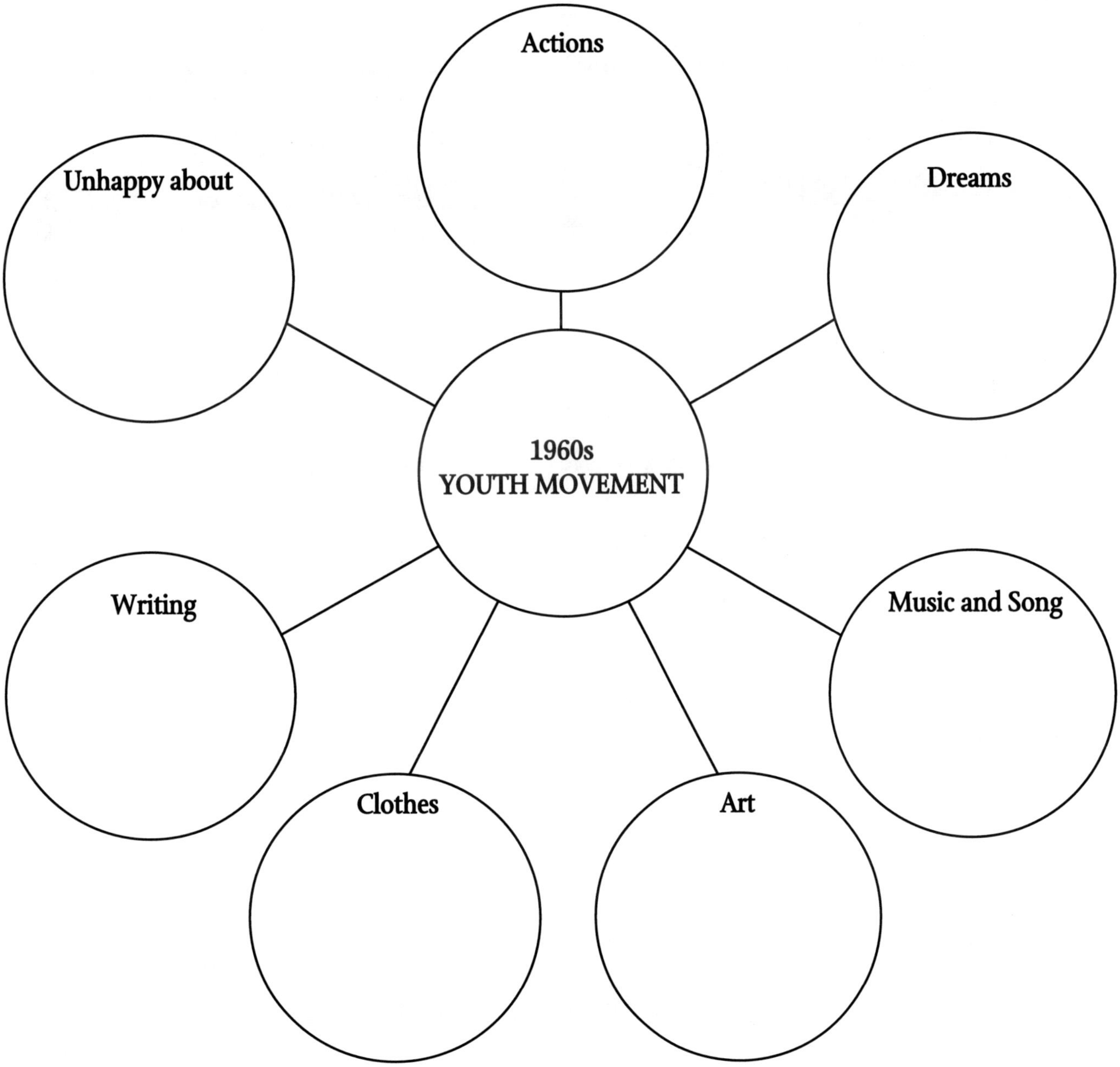

Actions

Unhappy about

Dreams

1960s
YOUTH MOVEMENT

Writing

Music and Song

Clothes

Art

NAME:

UNIT 4 • ACTIVITY 74
Death in the 1960s

Read these articles. Find out more about each man and these events. Then answer the questions.

Malcolm X Killed

NEW YORK CITY—Malcolm X was shot and killed today, February 21, 1965. He had recently left the Nation of Islam, an organization fighting for racial equality. He founded his own party. The men who shot him did not agree with his ideas.

Robert Kennedy Dies

LOS ANGELES—Robert Kennedy won the California primary for president. After Kennedy spoke to supporters on June 4, 1968, in Los Angeles, Sirhan Sirhan shot him. He was upset with Kennedy's support for Israel. Kennedy died two days later.

President Kennedy Assassinated

DALLAS, Texas—President John F. Kennedy was shot today, November 22, 1963. He was in a motorcade when shots rang out. He died a short while later. Lee Harvey Oswald was captured and charged with the crime.

Martin Luther King Shot and Killed

MEMPHIS, Tennessee—Civil Rights leader and Nobel Prize winner Dr. Martin Luther King, Jr., was shot and killed today, April 4, 1968. He was supporting striking garbage workers.

1. In what years did these deaths happen? ______________________________

2. What did all these deaths have in common? ______________________________

____

3. What was something different about each one? ______________________________

____

4. What problems in America concerned these men? ______________________________

____

5. How did each man influence American history? ______________________________

____

6. How do you think Americans reacted to each of these deaths? ______________________________

____

UNIT 4 • ACTIVITY 75
The Vietnam War

Read the paragraphs about the Vietnam War. Use the facts and details listed in the box to complete the sentences below.

South Vietnam	protest	Vietcong	so much help	U. S. government
Southeast Asia	escalated	Nixon	communist	took over South Vietnam

Vietnam is in **1.** ______________________. The French left Vietnam in 1954. Vietnam was divided into two countries. North Vietnam had a **2.** ______________________ government. South Vietnam did not. The United States helped **3.** ______________________ because it did not want communism to spread. The **4.** ______________________ fought against South Vietnam.

President Kennedy sent some help to South Vietnam. President Johnson wanted to win the war. He **5.** ______________________, or increased, the help America sent. Not all Americans believed the United States should send Vietnam **6.** ______________________. Many began to **7.** ______________________. Television reports from Vietnam showed something different from what the **8.** ______________________ was saying. Finally, President **9.** ______________________ pulled American troops out of Vietnam. He also increased American bombing in the area. In 1973, all America's military left Vietnam. In 1975, North Vietnam **10.** ______________________. America did not stop communism or North Vietnam.

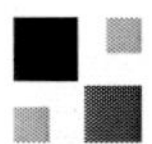

NAME:

UNIT 4 • ACTIVITY 76
Watergate

Watergate was an important event. Read about it in reference material or on the Internet. Then number each event in each set of events. Write 1 before the one that happened first. Write 2 before the next one. Continue until all four are numbered. Then do the next set.

Set 1

_______ President Nixon stopped the FBI investigation.

_______ Five men were arrested at the Democratic National Committee headquarters in the Watergate Building.

_______ The burglars went to jail.

_______ Washington Post reporters Woodward and Bernstein began investigating the break-in.

Set 2

_______ President Nixon refused to hand over tape recordings to the Senate.

_______ President Nixon ordered a cover-up.

_______ The courts demanded the president turn over the tape recordings.

_______ A Senate committee began to investigate.

Set 3

_______ The House of Representatives passed three charges against President Nixon.

_______ The tape recordings showed President Nixon planned the cover-up.

_______ President Nixon resigned.

_______ The House of Representatives investigated grounds to impeach President Nixon.

NAME:

UNIT 4 • ACTIVITY 77
Who Supported What

Since 1964, the presidents have had many ideas. They did different things. Find out about these presidents and what they did. Read each sentence. Then write the presidents' names that complete the sentences correctly.

President Lyndon Johnson	President Ronald Reagan
President Bill Clinton	President George W. Bush

1. The government under ______________________________ had high government spending on the Vietnam War and Great Society Programs.
2. The government under ______________________________ increased Cold War military spending and cut spending on social programs.
3. The government under ______________________________ began Medicare and Medicaid programs.
4. ______________________________ and ______________________________ pushed hard for large tax breaks for the rich.
5. ______________________________ and ______________________________ took a strong stand against communism.
6. ______________________________ and ______________________________ supported NAFTA.
7. ______________________________ wanted major changes to American healthcare, but Congress would not support changes.
8. ______________________________ and ______________________________ supported the conservative ideas of the New Right.
9. Under ______________________________, the government had a budget surplus.
10. ______________________________ shut down the government when Congress let the government run out of money.

NAME:

UNIT 4 • ACTIVITY 78
America Today

Every ten years, the United States takes a census. The census counts people in the country. It also asks people many questions. Then the results are put together. They describe America and how it has changed over ten years.

Choose a state. Use census figures to answer these questions about that state. Compare your answers with those of someone who researched another state. You can find information at www.census.gov.

State: ______________________________

1. What is its most recent population? ____________
2. What was its population in another year? ____________
3. How did its population change? ____________
4. What is its birthrate? ____________
5. What is the average income of its people? ____________
6. What is the percentage of its people who completed high school? ____________
7. What is the percentage of its people who are unemployed? ____________
8. What is the percentage of its people who live in poverty? ____________

NAME:

UNIT 4 • ACTIVITY 79
Technology Today

Technology has changed our lives. It is changing them faster and faster. More and more parts of our lives are influenced by technology. Each clue on the puzzle is about today's technology. Use the words listed in the box and the clues below to fill in the puzzle.

credit	computers	videos	games	Internet
station	microwave	televisions	drugs	heart

Across

3. In the 1980s, bands started making music ________________.
4. The consumer culture grew fast after ________________ cards became popular.
7. Today, ________________ are involved in every part of our life.
8. Doctors are now able to transplant a(n) ________________ into someone who needs it.
9. Many children play video ________________ rather than play outside.
10. The Russians and Americans share a space ________________.

Down

1. In the kitchen, a(n) ________________ now heats food very quickly.
2. The first ________________ were black and white, while later ones had color pictures.
5. Today, many computers are connected through the ________________.
6. Researchers discovered miracle ________________ that have saved many lives.

NAME:

UNIT 4 • ACTIVITY 80
September 11

Use the words listed in the box to complete the paragraphs below. They tell about events that have happened since September 2001.

World Trade Center	Al Qaeda	Middle East	Pentagon
Afghanistan	Islam	9–11	War on Terrorism
Iraq	western	terrorists	weapons of mass destruction

America was attacked on September 11, 2001. That day is often called **1.** ____________________. The attacks took place in New York City and Washington, D.C. **2.** ____________________ flew airplanes into two **3.** ____________________ buildings. They also flew a plane into the **4.** ____________________. Another plane was crashed into the ground in Pennsylvania before it could reach its target. More than two thousand people died in these attacks.

President George W. Bush called for a(n) **5.** ____________________. He sent the military into **6.** ____________________. The leaders of **7.** ____________________ lived there. They had planned these attacks. Then, in 2003, the President sent troops into **8.** ____________________. He sent them to look for **9.** ____________________. This country was soon split. Different sides were fighting for power.

The religion of most people in these countries is **10.** ____________________. Some of them have very strong religious beliefs. They do not want **11.** ____________________ ways in their country. That is one reason why they act against the United States. They are also against American actions in the **12.** ____________________. This area has many problems. What has happened recently?